The Magic Carpet Ride

To Feel Is to See, to See Is to Feel

CRYSTAL DUNN

BALBOA.
PRESS
A DIVISION OF HAY HOUSE

Balboa Press books may be ordered through booksellers or by contacting:

Balboa Press
A Division of Hay House
1663 Liberty Drive
Bloomington, IN 47403
www.balboapress.com.au
1 (877) 407-4847

Because of the dynamic nature of the Internet, any web addresses or links contained in this book may have changed since publication and may no longer be valid. The views expressed in this work are solely those of the author and do not necessarily reflect the views of the publisher, and the publisher hereby disclaims any responsibility for them.

The author of this book does not dispense medical advice or prescribe the use of any technique as a form of treatment for physical, emotional, or medical problems without the advice of a physician, either directly or indirectly. The intent of the author is only to offer information of a general nature to help you in your quest for emotional and spiritual well-being. In the event you use any of the information in this book for yourself, which is your constitutional right, the author and the publisher assume no responsibility for your actions.

Any people depicted in stock imagery provided by Thinkstock are models,
and such images are being used for illustrative purposes only.
Certain stock imagery © Thinkstock.

Print information available on the last page.

ISBN: 978-1-4525-2866-3 (sc)
ISBN: 978-1-4525-2867-0 (e)

Balboa Press rev. date: 05/04/2015

Crystal Dunns' Journey through life has been both challenging and rewarding. It is wonderful too meet such a person who has walked the fine line that many of us have walked. That of service in the face of seemingly insurmountable challenges.

The depth of passion within Crystal is revealed in this challenging story she has penned. The mark of truth and dedication is evident at every turn of the page.

Her journey reflects much that we find within us all as we search for our spiritual roots.

Crystal has rendered an invaluable service working with those who cannot live a life of freedom, bound within the constraints of care and protection.

Reading her story it soon becomes evident that within the selfless service to others, there has always been space for her pursuit of the esoteric and the spiritual.

Crystal can carry on her challenging journey through life with the re assurance that there are many out there that admire and honor who she is.

Gary Cook. DSc. KTJ. Author and Researcher.

Prologue

I have written this book to help others understand how important their vibrational energy is. It determines our outlook, our attractions to self & our ability to manifest our future. It can open doors of higher learning or shut us in dark places that only self-belief can free us from. Finding balance within, can be challenging to sustain & blossom. When we have found this state for ourselves, it is easier to recognize that which does not serve us well. This gives us the strength to nurture ourselves while discerning the nature around us

About the author page

Crystal Dunn is an energy healer, artist, and spiritual mentor. She is passionate about creating an elevated environment whereby understanding and direction can be established for a powerful yet softly caring and loving healing of the mind and soul. Crystal utilizes practical skills and common sense to raise inner awareness through self-development.

Dedication Page

This book is dedicated to all those on a spiritual path, who have ever doubted their inner knowing. To those who have felt isolated, alone, or confused, because of what they feel and see to be true. To the one's that sense the esoteric depths of life, once the superficial layers of existence fall away, thus opening us up to the endless dreaming's of tomorrow. This awareness shows us that reality is determined by the ability to open or close our consciousness.

Acknowledgements Page

My acknowledgements go to the select few that offered support, friendship, and spiritual mentoring, that was needed for me to believe in myself.

Their inspiration, acceptance, and tutoring in self-truth, helped me to appreciate my difference as a gift.

Heartfelt respect and honour go to my spiritual family of the Pureora forest, who welcomed me into their world as a sister.

The unforgettable Wiremu Turner who conveyed the importance in life through story and sacred teachings from Aotearoa, New Zealand. May you run free, like the child that reflected in your eyes.

Deep appreciation to Gary Cook for endorsing my book, being a friend, and sharing sparkle where ever you walked.

Sincere love and thanks to the Beauchamp family for holding me close when personal dreams faded. Without your love and belief, I would not have the courage to write this book.

Namaste

Introduction Page

I was born a sensitive. I had the gift of feeling and seeing the world from an uncommon depth. This ensured a life of magical proportions. From youth to adulthood, I have shared within this book, the ups and downs of my heart-opening lessons. These experiences have directed my spiritual course.

Charter my childhood through a parallel world with the supernatural. Let me show you that a child's imagination is a reality we need not grow out of.

I give you the evidence to connect childhood belief with adult knowing.

Follow the understandings I gain in human nature while working as a carer and mentor for those with limited independence.

I showcase the synchronicities, supernatural, and at times scariness of my timeline. Lastly I engage you in a spiritual adventure from Australia to Aotearoa, New Zealand. This is where all I felt and knew became cemented. Fall in love, get to know Maori traditions and culture. Meet the Patupaiarehe, also known as the Faerie folk or little people that are multi-dimensional beings living deep in the forest.

Chapter 1

I grew up on the Mornington Peninsula, across the road from Port Phillip Bay. I am the youngest of five to a solo mum. The house we lived in was built in 1858 by H G Chapman as one of the first guesthouses in service to the ever-growing port harbour. It had a large veranda out front, as well as four bedrooms, an attic, and a cellar. The lounge room had an open fire and the kitchen had a warm pot belly stove. The bathroom grew a cluster of mushrooms each winter. The outside toilet housed a wonderful array of different sized daddy long leg spiders. The laundry adjacent to the toilet had the original concrete double basins with our equally nostalgic wringer washing machine. It was on a quarter acre block scattered with fruit trees of crab-apple, fig, lemon, and blood plum. The shed was as old as the house, made of corrugated iron with a rusty holed roof. Life was simple yet not care free.

This was where I first recall being visited at night by beings not of this world. This phenomenon started from as young as I can remember. The nights they came I would be awoken by their presence. I was too scared to open my eyes, for once I saw them everything would change. Spontaneously I would not be in my bed anymore. The round purple rug in my room would be floating above blackness, with me in the middle and a group of beings around me. I remember watching a movie screen where my window used to be. I was shown pictures of a boy around the same age as me. I felt a bond with him like a brother. I felt content when I saw him on screen. Next thing I knew I would wake up on my purple rug; the floor was back underneath me and I was in my room. It was tricky jumping from my rug to the bed, in case the floor disappeared again. I thought of running to mums bed, but I was too petrified that there would be no floor to stand on between my bed and the door. This was when I would usually wet the bed, as I was too scared to move. The warmth comforted me long enough to fall asleep. On the nights the beings didn't show up I would wake, sense for any movement, if it was clear I would throw my bedclothes off and run as fast as I could down the hall to jump into mums bed. Once in her bed I didn't feel safe until I was touching her, with my foot, arm, or even just one finger. I thought as long as we were touching, Mum would wake up if they tried to take me. I could then relax knowing I was safe and undisturbed. This went on for many years along with the embarrassment of bed-wetting. I had a plastic mattress protector that crumpled when it was sat on, letting everyone know that I wet the bed.

Mum tried numerous incentives to prevent me from wetting the bed, no drinks after dinner, and a present if I did not wet the bed for a week. I got a couple of presents, but little did mum know that on those particular weeks I didn't get visited at night. I never knew when they would show up. There were times between visits when I almost forgot about them. I thought it must have been a dream. I lived in one world by day and another at night.

My mother started to become progressively ill with Agra phobia. She spent numerous days in bed and was unable to leave the house for fear of crowds and wide open spaces. This left me to fend for myself because my teenage siblings were not home a lot of the time. I didn't understand why mum couldn't get up out of bed. I remember going for long adventures on my bike, mainly to the beach. I would experience the magic in my day and excitably return home for dinner. It was not until I saw mum that I remembered she was sick. I had no one to share my story of the day. With one look at her, my excitement turned to despair. as I wondered what to do.

I don't remember eating or even feeling hungry, just the puzzlement and my lack of understanding of my mother's condition. One morning an ambulance arrived to take mum to hospital. She said goodbye to me and told me not to worry. She said she would be back soon, when she was all better. I felt hollow and thought she would be back the next day. I woke in the night and ran to mums room, only to find her bed empty. I was bewildered as to why she was not in her bed. I knew she was in hospital, but I wondered why she was not home yet. The house was empty, with not a soul to be found. I went out the front to look for her, for anyone. I gazed down the road both ways but no one was there. I stood under the streetlight and cried, "Mum, mum, where are you?" This felt like forever as my emotions built up to hysteria. I had never felt so alone before. I noticed three figures in the distance. I kept yelling out for mum as they drew closer. It was dark and the only light was that of the street lamp I stood under. I became frightened as they drew closer. I heard them yell out my name, but I could not recognize them. I yelled out again for mum, and got a reply "It is Kathy". The other two figures were my brothers. I was so relieved to see them. They had gone to the shops while I was sleeping, not knowing I would wake. Not long after this happened I was sent to the house of my eldest sister Patricia. She lived in the country with her husband and two young daughters. It was decided I would stay with them until mum was well enough to have me back. I was timid, even though my sister and her family spent most holidays with us. Everything was different when I lived with them. I had so many new restraints and boundaries I was not used to.

My sister got word mum was coming out of hospital a few months later. Arrangements were made for me to return home. I felt blank. No butterflies or feelings of excitement. I wanted to go home more than anything but I couldn't shake the feeling of when I last saw mum. She was so sick she didn't even notice me. I wouldn't believe she was better until I saw her again. When I saw her, she was smiling and gave me the warmest hug. This showed me that she was all better. Mum became involved with the local community again, helping wayward mothers and their children find strength and purpose.

Chapter 2

My childhood became filled with many supernatural experiences that became normal for me.

At the age of five I remember playing on my two seated swing in the back yard, pushing it to and fro with my imaginary friend. I was mesmerized at how I could stop pushing and come to a halt, then my imaginary friend could make the swing move to and fro again. The delight of playing with someone no one else could see was elating. A thought crossed my mind, a test. I said out loud "If you are real you will push". There was no movement. My imaginary friend then got up from the swing. I ran after him saying "No, I am sorry". I started to cry. My imaginary friend said "I will come back one day". "You can't leave it was just a game", I said. He walked a few steps away and then vanished.

Years later as an adult in my late twenties' I visited my sister Kathy for a cuppa and a chat. We got talking about the imaginary friend I had when I was little. She said "You totally believed he was real, you even gave him a name". Perplexed I asked "What was his name"? She said "Pat". The memory of my mum's uncle Pat came flooding to my conscience. My mother had a photo of him on her dressing table, of which I would stare at as a little girl. Now I knew why, it was him all along, not imaginary. He was my guardian angel. This gave me solace in my connection to him.

By the age of six I was walking to and from primary school on my own. One beautiful clear day I saw an elderly couple walking up the street towards me. They had different colours around them, which pulsed and charged with each movement. I wondered where their colours came from. When I arrived home I told mum what I had seen. She explained that they *were called auras and that people have different colours around them. I asked why? "You are seeing their energy it is a special thing to see", she said.*

Kathy who was nine years older than me, overheard what had happened on my way home from school that day. Mum asked Kathy to go to the shops for her. Kathy asked if I wanted to come. I said "Yes", excitably. I was happy to go to the shops with my big sister. We had just got out the gate and a person came toward us, my sister asked "What colour is that person". I was puzzled at her request, looking in her face for answers. I said nothing. Another person walked past. "What colour are they", she asked again. A hard feeling was in my chest, I answered "I don't know". My sister asked the same question of each passer-by until we returned home. I didn't want to see the colours anymore and I didn't after that.

I found it hard to make friends as a child because of how sensitive I was to the feelings of people and my surroundings. I managed to befriend one girl named Tara. I asked her over to my house after school one afternoon to play. I loved to draw, so we got out paper and pencils to sit down at the double desk in my room. I had two single beds in my room, opposite each other, up against the wall. One of the single beds was for guests, which adorned my large selection of toys. The desk was opposite the window giving us a view of the two single beds and the whole room. We were drawing away when Tara said "I feel funny". I instinctively knew what she was feeling. I said "It is ok, it is just the other little girl that lives here, if we are quiet, we might see her". We sat quietly, intently looking at where we felt the funny energy. The bed with all my toys on showed an indentation, like the weight of a person sitting on it. My favourite toy was a Miss Piggy doll, made of latex rubber. She had wire through her arms and legs to enable movement. Before our eyes we saw one of Miss Piggy's arms slowly bend upwards. We looked at each other excitably. I noted an ounce of terror in Tara's eyes. Then the other arm also raised up. Just at that moment mum walked into the room to see how we were. The little girl's presence disappeared. I told my mother we were busy so that she would not stay long. Tara asked "Where has the little girl gone?" I replied "I did not know, she just comes to play sometimes".

I made another special friend at primary school a boy named Gerald. We didn't meet until a few years later when I was eight years old. We would spend our weekends together, riding our bikes, walking our dogs along the beach, and looking for adventures. One day we decided to hang out at my house, seeing as no one was home. We sat in the lounge room and talked. At the other end of the room was a long wooden cabinet. Mum had many framed pictures hanging on the walls above it. For some reason I started talking about my grandmother who had passed away before I was born. Gerald asked "Are you ok". I replied "Yes why". He said "There are tears coming from your eyes". "I don't feel sad, I think it is my grandmother", I said. In that instant there were four loud thuds on the wooden cabinet. Gerald and I ran for our lives to mum's work. We saw that the community house where mum worked was closed. Gerald said "I am due home, are you going to be alright?" I replied "Yes, but I am not going into my house if mum's not there". I got home and stood at the gate. I yelled out for mum. "Mum are you home?" I heard mums voice yell back "Yes". I ran down the corridor yelling out "Where are you". She replied, "I am in the kitchen". I looked at her in fright. Mum asked "What is wrong?" I told her about the four loud thuds on the cabinet. I explained that Gerald and I were talking about grandma, when tears started to well in my eyes, and it was after this we heard the thuds. Mum tried to be rational saying "One of the pictures probably fell off the wall". I was adamant and said "No if it was a picture that fell off the wall it would just go thud once, not four times". Mum said "Well let's go and have a look". There was no sign of a disturbance. There were no fallen pictures, or anything to explain what Gerald and I had heard. Mum said not to worry about it as she was home now. This was comforting to a point, but it still did not explain what had happened.

When renovating the front room, a pair of children's shoes were found in one of the walls near the front door. In the 18th and 19th century, it was believed that children's shoes hidden near openings of the house would ward off evil spirits. Many things went missing in that house, particularly anything that was a pair, yet only one item would be taken. By the time I was twelve we left this haunted house. I had become accustomed to the energies that lived there with us. Kathy also felt strangely attached to them. I still remember the day we left. Both of us shed a tear, as we said goodbye to the house.

Chapter 3

When I hit teenage years my bizarre childhood experiences couldn't have been further from my mind. Puberty set in and I became emotionally self-absorbed. At the age of nineteen I had my first vision. This was where my history with unusual phenomena resurfaced. I was basking in the summer sun. My mind drifts off and plays a vision like a movie. Full colour and emotion grab my attention.

I am in the Australian outback walking up an embankment of dusty, rocky, red ground. I am not alone. A small group of people I feel familiar to, are walking in the same direction. There is a moving sense between us as we reach the top and peer across the valley below. There are two red suns above us creating an ember like glow. We are all there for the same reason. All drawn to this energy field we are looking at. Embarking back down the cliff, I am ushered by a male voice saying "Don't forget the templates". I look down to see a rock bullion with ancient writing carved into it like that of hieroglyphics. "Don't forget the templates" the voice ushers again. I pick up the rock and it disappears into my hand, becoming part of me. The sensation of picking it up and holding it, has not left me since that day.

At the age of twenty-one I went on a holiday up north in search of a warmer climate and more fun. I found a job waitressing and I met some of my favourite people, which I am still friends with to this day. I worked night's waitressing and by day attended tertiary education studying fashion design. I found a house to rent that was advertised in the local paper. It read - wanted a caretaker of one hundred and thirty acre property, while the owner travels overseas. (Free rent). I arranged a meeting with the owner to view the property. I asked my friend Isa to come. She also brought along her young son. It was nestled in the hinterland twenty minutes away from *where I worked. On our way there we passed a quaint little plant nursery. We stopped in to have a look. We followed the path to a small cottage nestled amongst all the plants, trees, and shrubs, for sale. We peered inside the window, through majestic deep purple curtains to see crystals and trinkets for sale. There was a man pottering about the nursery, so I asked him about the opening hours of the cottage. He said that the lady who runs the cottage is only open part-time, and probably best to give her a ring to make an appointment. The man got one of her pamphlets for me. The pamphlet said that she did tarot readings and spiritual advancement courses. Isa and I were both interested, as neither of us had experienced a tarot reading before. We decided to give this lady a ring to arrange an appointment when we returned home. We travelled on to view the rental property. The driveway was easy to overlook as it was just a small cutting that blended well into treed bush land. The driveway wound round a gully in an s-shape with a twelve metre drop on one side. The house was five kilometres away from the main road. It was perched next to a deep, wide valley, with a high embankment. Isa's young son said that he didn't like the feeling of the place. We both brushed it off as him feeling uncomfortable in the new surroundings. The owner's name was Bruce. He was nice enough, and in his early fifties'. He explained that he annually went overseas to obtain artefacts for his shop. He said "Everything is for sale in Asia". He stated that as long as you have enough money to make a replica of the object you want, you can import ancient relics. I was amazed by this statement, and a little put off his character because of it. He escorted us around the property in his four-wheel drive. The main job on the property was to check and regulate the water levels of two dams. This was done manually with a floater valve. It all seemed straight forward enough, so I accepted the challenge. We went back to the house for a cup of tea and a chat. The house was hand built. It was made out of the most beautifully coloured wood. The smell of the wood was divine, along with its character. We sat out on the wide veranda which overlooked the valley below. I asked if it would be ok to have my dog on the property. Bruce said that would be fine. He let me know there was a horse living on the property but not to worry as it looks after itself. He then out of nowhere, asked "Do you believe in the supernatural?" I replied "Yes why do you ask?" Bruce went on to tell me that he feels there was an old Aboriginal burial ground not far from the house. He said "I didn't know about it until*

I started excavating for the house plot, I found some old artefacts which are in my room upstairs". He said, "The room you will be staying in is next to mine". He asked that I didn't touch anything in his room, especially the artefacts. I gave him my assurance that I would not intrude on his personal space. I asked to look upstairs at the room I would be staying in. There were two bedrooms upstairs, with a studio overlooking the valley. An inspirational setting to do my arts and crafts. He showed me a unique musical instrument from Far East Asia that reminded me of a glockenspiel. It consisted of three thin metal bars at different horizontal levels. The bars held eight, large hollowed out nuts. There was a slit going halfway through each nut to create a percussion sound when hit. The varied size of the nuts, gave off a wonderful variation of sound. He went on to tell me of the last caretaker on the property. A woman in her thirties who read tarot cards and believed in the supernatural. He said "The woman saw an Aboriginal man on the veranda". "A real person", I asked. "No the ghost of one", he replied. I think to myself, I am not feeling comfortable about accepting to look after this property anymore. He went on to say "The woman invited the Aboriginal man into the house". I sat there flabbergasted, wondering what he was going to say next. He said "It is ok, I got rid of him from inside the house, just don't invite him in again". I said "You don't have to worry about me doing that". He said "You may see him from time to time standing on the veranda, he won't bother you, as long as you don't invite him in". I said "No way, I am not that silly, I can't believe that woman did invite him in, crazy". He asked "Are you still interested in moving in". I accepted the offer, as it was a beautiful rustic home with the most captivating views, plus free rent.

I rang my mother to tell her the news. I filled her in about the story of the Aboriginal man. I told her that this was my only apprehension about moving in. I asked her what to do if I saw him. Mum said "Do not give him any of your energy, just ignore him, and occupy yourself with something that keeps your mind busy". That was when I had the idea to start my poetry book. I have been writing poetry since I was eleven years old. I decided when I had settled into the new house, I would go through all of my poems and pick the best ones.

I rang the tarot card lady to book a reading for myself and Isa. We got an appointment at 10am the next morning. I picked up Isa and we made *our way anxiously to the nursery cottage. On our way there Isa told me of a reoccurring dream. It involved her boyfriend's best friend. She said "He keeps appearing in my dreams as a knight coming to take me away on horseback, I would never do anything with him, but I cannot shake off this knight in shining armour dream". I asked if she had any hidden feelings for him. She said "He is attractive but that is it". She declared how strong her love is for her boyfriend. I said "Well don't worry about it then, you are not doing anything wrong, after all it is just a dream". We laughed. You could see this dream troubled Isa.*

We made a pact to not give anything away at the tarot reading, by keeping our answers, and body language, to a minimum. I remember mum telling me it is not good to know too much about your future. Mum advised me to stay away from tarot cards. In the same respect, I thought it is the choices we make that change our future.

We were welcomed inside by the tarot reader named Greta. The room was like a den, shadowed by the bushes that surrounded it. Candles were placed precisely to highlight important ornaments and create sparkle from hanging crystals. Within minutes the noise of the traffic outside faded. I felt like I was in a time zone all my own. Greta asked who would like to go first. I looked at Isa, and she looked at me. "I will", Isa said. Phew! I thought, let's just see how this is done.

Greta asked Isa to shuffle the cards and stop when she was ready to hand them back. Greta then lay the cards in a varied sequence. She commenced to tell Isa that she was in love with a man, but there is another man frequenting your dreams. He is close to you and your current love. He is wondering if he has a chance with you, or should he stay a dream. Isa said she would not hurt her current boyfriend. Greta smiled and said "Well once you believe this, these dreams of him coming to sweep you off your feet will stop".

Isa and I looked at each other in amazement. Isa had not told anyone about her dream. I was the first to know. How did Greta know? It was my turn. Ok I shuffle the cards, then stop. I handed the cards back to Greta. I was doing my best poker face and trying not to think of anything at all. Greta starts describing a boy, who is tall, with blue eyes. She said "You care for him, but more out of duty". "I see another boy, there is a spark, he is making you question your relationship". "You will have to choose between the two". I replied "Thank you, I know". What she said was spot on for both of us, it blew us away. We contained our excitement until we left. Neither of us had experienced anything like it. So if anyone I knew needed guidance, or was troubled about their future, I sent them to Greta for a reading. I was amazed at how many of my friends benefitted from her open direction.

I moved onto the property a week later with my dog Lucy. I became accustomed to the isolation of the area by getting in tune with the nature around me. Sunsets were spectacular from the veranda, the bird calls, and the wind in the trees, echoing through the valley below. I couldn't ignore the uneasy feeling I got on dusk. I wasn't sure if it was the story I had been told of the Aboriginal man, or the fact I was there alone in the ever approaching dark. Either way I relished in the beauty, sights, and smells, of my new surroundings. I decided to capture what I saw, with paint on canvas. I would walk all over the property looking for different plants to paint. Almost a month had passed and I was feeling a lot more comfortable. One evening I was admiring the setting sun from the lounge room that overlooked the veranda. I saw an Aboriginal man out the corner of my eye. He was standing on the veranda looking out across the valley. He stood with one leg raised and his body resting sideways on a tall spear. I did not want to double take my gaze in case I welcomed his gaze in return. I sat pretending not to see him. I focused my mind on thoughts of anything else but him. I felt frozen in time. His image faded with the setting sun. Phew! The night fell into darkness with nothing around me for miles. The once secluded serenity now seemed sparked with fright. My room was upstairs and far away from what I just saw. I decided to go to bed and read for a while, trying to go to sleep. I managed to get to sleep after reading for a short while. I woke a few hours later in the pitch dark to a screeching noise. It was like nothing I had ever heard before. I thought I must be brave to get up and turn on the light. I mustered the courage to get up and walk the three steps to the light switch. With the light on, I saw nothing that could make such a noise. I hopped back into bed armed with my torch. Just as I was calming to sleep the noise started again. I focused my hearing on where it was coming from. It was next to the bed. I turned on the torch to light up the noise. To my surprise I found two Gecko's wrestling on the floor. What a delightful relief, nothing to fear. I could now rest. I woke to the most glorious day. It was full of colour, *in dawn hues, with the smell of the wood permeating throughout the house. I was surrounded by nature as far as the eye could see and just me, magic.*

Today I would investigate my surroundings. I started by looking at the relics upstairs. I knew I shouldn't, but once near them I felt compelled to touch a white hammer-like tool made of stone. I touched it with only one finger to feel its coldness. A cool breeze went up my elbow. I backed off, deciding to leave the artefacts alone. Some areas of the property had the same cool feeling, especially near one of the man-made dams. I never did see the horse that lived on the property. I did hear it galloping by from time to time. I was tired and hungry from my trek around the property, so I made my way back to the house. The light started to fade. I remembered what I had seen on the veranda the night before. I decided to let that thought go and told myself that the Aboriginal folk were here long before me. Night fell and I was relieved to not see the apparition of the Aboriginal man again. I got my journal from upstairs and sat in the dining room to write. I dreamt of all the adventure I would have on the property. This dream was shaken abruptly by the sound of the glockenspiel instrument upstairs playing by itself. I tremored at the thought. I rang my mum who had also dealt with unusual phenomenon in her life. Mum explained that the best thing I could do was ignore it. "How", I said. The image of the Aboriginal man outside on the veranda was fine as he was outside, but now something was inside playing a physical instrument. Mum said "It feeds off your energy, so the more you think about it the more energy you give it". Mum asked "Is there anything else I could focus on". I thought, my journal, my poetry, to organize my writings, in order to make a book. That was my mission at dusk until bedtime from that night on. Not long after this happened, I didn't like being alone on the property anymore. The owner was not due back for a few months. I asked Wayne a male friend from work, if he would like to stay with me for free rent. He jumped at the chance of living rent free. I didn't tell him what I had experienced out there. I don't think he would have believed me if I had. I didn't want to jeopardise my chances of having company. It took a couple of days before he was able to move in. I did my darnedest to keep my mind busy, especially at dusk. The night before Wayne arrived I was busy clearing and cleaning to make room. It turned dark before I knew it. I wanted something easy for dinner, so I decided to make a toasted sandwich in the electric sandwich maker. My dog Lucy started barking her head off, at what, I don't know. It was pitch black outside. I heard her running down the drive chasing something. I felt safe. Whatever it was, she was chasing away. I plugged in the sandwich maker to have it blow all the power out in the house. This left me in complete darkness. I could still hear Lucy way down the drive barking. When you are in this sort of situation all your senses become heightened. I told myself to stay calm and think of where I had seen a candle. I instantly remembered the one on the table and that a box of matches were next to the stove. I fumbled and found the matches, and then the candle to light. Once I had minimal light, I had to go down stairs under the house to switch the electrical mains back on. I got the torch from my bedroom upstairs, which was frightening enough, next door to the instrument that played by itself. I had to quickly fade that thought out if I was to assert myself to the job at hand. I put the candle back on the table and proceeded out the front door. It was eerie to say the least. I could no longer hear Lucy. As much as I called, she was nowhere to be seen. I could easily find where I was going with the torch in front of me. It was the areas behind and beside me that the torch did not illuminate, which spooked me the most. I got under the house and found the power box. Sure enough the mains switch had thrown itself off. I flicked the switch back on, but there was no light coming from the house. I couldn't do anything else. I had done what I set out to do, to no avail. The only thing I could think of was to ring the electrical company. I was worried about Lucy as it was way to quiet. I rang the electrical company to find that the houses in my area are metred from the poles along the roadside. This meant that the problem would not be looked at until the following day. Well as you can imagine, by this stage I was wide awake. There was no way I would be able to rest my eyelids. I stayed up until dawn writing and sorting through my poetry. When daylight broke, I was happily exhausted to see the sun. I went out onto the veranda to find Lucy curled up on her bed. All good I can get some rest now, I thought. The next few months were fun with Wayne staying. I got to learn how to ride a motorbike. This made it so much easier getting around the property to check the dams. I dug a vegetable garden and considered what I would grow for the season. Next minute I saw a car coming down the drive. It was Bruce. He explained that his trip had been cut short. I was flabbergasted at the thought of him staying next to me upstairs. He said that he would be happy to stay in the caravan outside. I felt relieved. I introduced Wayne to Bruce. I informed Bruce that I became scared on my own, so I asked my friend Wayne to keep me company.

Bruce smiled. He seemed fine with the situation. I woke the next morning to hear Bruce downstairs. I imagined what it would feel like being home again after months away. I decided to give him space to reacquaint himself that morning. I got dressed to work in the garden. I was still defining the garden beds, as to how big. I saw Bruce watching through the kitchen window. I smiled and waved to him. I got a blank look in response. I had a break and went inside to make a cup of tea. Bruce said "I think it would be best if you moved out". I was shocked. He had just watched me shovelling the garden beds. I thought this is the thanks I get. Disgruntled I said "Ok, but I will have to find somewhere else to live first". He said "Take as much time as you need". I spoke to Wayne when he got back from work about the situation. He knew a couple who were looking for a house sitter when they went down south to work for the snow season. They lived just down the road. It seemed brilliant, and too easy.

Chapter 4

Wayne introduced me to Sven and Kate. They were laidback and easy to talk to. Kate took me outside to meet their three horses. I had never looked after horses before and I was quite timid. Kate gave out a whistle, and they came cantering down from high in the paddocks to greet us. They were similar to dogs, I thought to myself. I was shown their food and what to mix for their daily feed. I became accustomed to them by giving them a brush. I was warned not to stand at the back of them in case they were frisky and tried to kick me. Life was good. All had fallen into place once more. I went for a drive with Wayne just a short distance away to meet some other friends of his. There were many dirt roads out in the country where we lived. This one in particular was well driven, with many hooks, turns, and corners. There were hand-made signs nailed on trees in remembrance of all the people who had an accident on the road. I was perplexed to witness a lot of the people were related, like Gerald Scott, Thomas Scott, etc. Wayne also thought it was a rally track, sliding his car around the corners. The corners in most cases, were only wide enough to fit one car. God help us if another car was coming the other way. I pointed out the signs of previous accidents to him. "It was not sensible to be driving so fanatically", I said. He laughed and replied "Don't worry". Yeah easy for him to say he was driving. I was a passenger with no control over what happens next. We made it safely to his friend's house. The house was quaint and made of sky blue weatherboard. It had a small veranda out front to view the surrounding cattle farm. We were greeted by a large vicious looking dog which was barking ferociously at the car. I was scared to get out. When the dog heard its owner's voice to back off, it turned into the most passive, gentle animal. I got along really well with Nadia and

Greg and their mate Travis, Wayne's friends. I visited them regularly. I was invited to attend the local markets with them one weekend. They had their own market stall. I decided to try and sell my hand-made rock necklaces. It was a fun day and I got to acquaint myself much better with them. I found out that Travis was a cook and worked at another market, a short distance up the road. Travis was tall, dark, and handsome. I felt more than friendship starting to form towards him. He was a musician, songwriter, and carver. He invited me out the following Friday, to pick up food supplies for the market that coming weekend. I had a lovely time shopping with him. I had worked up an appetite, looking at all the yummy food stuffs. He asked "Are you busy this afternoon. I said "No". "Good", he said. Travis told me about a lovely place in the country, not far away that he would like to show me. "That would be nice, but I am hungry", I said. He was kind enough to suggest we pack a picnic. We dropped off the produce for the coming weekend market, and made some snacks for our country destination. We were ten minutes into our drive when Travis asked if I would mind if he stopped at a lookout coming up. I accepted, while thinking how romantic. I was just about to comment on the view when I noticed him pull out a needle and spoon from the centre console. I was shocked. I just stared at him. He asked if I wanted some. He said "It is speed". I said "No thanks". In my head all I could think of was how will he be able to drive the car. I didn't feel safe. I got out of the car, with a fake carefree attitude. I pretended that I wanted to get a better look at the view. All I had thought and felt about him was in a spin. I was hesitant to get back into the car. He then asked if I would like to drive. I said "Yeah ok". He directed me by saying "Just follow this road". I didn't know how to feel or what to say. Had he changed? I did not know.

I felt comfortable driving the car, a lot more than if Travis had driven. He started talking as normal. I felt relieved. I wondered why he needed to have the stuff if he just stayed the same. What did it do for him? Little did I know that this country drive was going to change my life? The car steering wheel became locked while I was trying to turn round a bend. Time was frozen. I no longer existed within this reality. All that was left was an overwhelming feeling of self. I was detached from sensation and stimulus. I had no control of the car. I saw an apparition of a male behind me, who whispered in my ear. Another male apparition was next to him, naked, sitting in an upright foetal position. He was rocking back and forth saying, "No", over and over, right before impact.

I then had no sense of self. I only knew I existed because of my observations. So many people walking in the same direction past me. One red headed man with his face so clear. I felt like I knew him but where from. Who are these people, I thought to myself. I woke up semi-conscious in hospital. I felt like I had blown in on a soft breeze, light and hazy. The voice of my sister Kathy untangles my dreamscape as her face became clearer. I am neither here nor there, because of the pain killing medication. The whole saga just feels like a dream I have woken from. In my semi-conscious state I tell my sister what I'd seen while in a coma. I don't remember much of what I was saying except the feeling. I recall an older lady wearing a purple shawl who helped bring me back to consciousness. My sister then handed me my clear quartz crystal. I took this crystal everywhere with me. It was with me the day of the car accident. I love crystals. By doing a technique called crystal gazing, images appear through the stones composition. This particular crystal looked like it had a wise man inside of it. A man with a long white beard and long white hair. I couldn't touch it, it felt horrible. It was now darkened at the bottom, like it had absorbed part of the impact. I told Kathy that it would need cleansing. It took almost two weeks before I could make sense of anything or find the strength to move. I would mentally talk to different parts of my body. "Wiggle your toes, raise your arms". There was a short space between the will of the mind and the action of the body. Luckily I came out of it relatively unscathed, well nothing that wouldn't heal to enable me full function again, in time. I suffered a severe blow to the head from hitting the steering wheel, breaking my jaw and facial bones. I also had a crushed L1 vertebrae. My mother was a mess. She was just thankful I was alive. Mum told me that when I was in intensive care, it seemed quite grim. My injuries were so severe there was a chance I wouldn't wake up again. Everyone was praying for me. Mum felt that the prayers changed my outcome. She recalled witnessing the severity of my injuries lift, by half before her eyes. It was then I woke up. After a little while I was getting the feeling back in my body. The catheter in me was becoming more and more uncomfortable. It got to the stage where I just wanted it out. The nurses said I would have to wait for the doctor to assess me first. The doctor came and assessed my physical capabilities. I was slow, but able. The doctor announced that the catheter could be taken out the next morning. The morning could not come quick enough. They took out the tubes and connected me to a mobile drip for pain relief. Any time I felt pain all I had to do was push the button. Travis came to visit that same day. I was happy to see that he was ok. He asked "Do you need anything. I replied "What I want more than anything is to go outside". He asked "Can you walk. I replied "Slowly". Travis helped me sit upright. I brought my legs around with my hands to dangle off the bed. I asked him to support me to stand. We strolled past the nurse's station and out the nearest exit. The sun was shining. "Oh the sun", I said. We sat down and had a good chat. He told me that when I was put into the ambulance I let out a gut wrenching scream. He said "I can't get that moment out of my head". I replied "I remember, I panicked as I thought if I got into the ambulance I was going to die". I told him that it wasn't his fault and that is why they are called accidents. After a long chat, Travis escorted me back to my bed. A nurse came rushing up to me asking "Where have you been"? I told her I had been outside in the sun. "You are ok that is the main thing", she said. My mother and sister were so upset, Mum was crying and Kathy angry. Kathy blasted me about how much this accident had affected our mum. Kathy said "She can't take anymore". I told her that I just wanted to go outside. I really didn't understand what all the fuss was about, I felt fine. Travis left not long after this. I asked one of the nurse's if she could assist me to take a shower. The nurse asked "Are you sure you are ready". I replied "Yes it would be nice to get properly clean". The nurse sat me down on a chair while she ran the shower. Before I hopped in I asked if I could see myself in the mirror. The nurse questioned again. "Are you sure you want to do that", she asked. I replied "Yes". Nothing prepared me for what I was about to see. My face was not my face anymore. The steering wheel had left many small imprinted circles across the right side of my forehead and cheek. My face was swollen beyond recognition. The whites of my eyes were like coloured marble. They reflected back at me the intensity of my internal injuries in many, bright red and blue, erratic lines. All this information abruptly relayed mentally in the moments before I collapsed. I explained to the nurse that I didn't know I was in such bad shape. I felt alright within myself until I saw my reflection. The nurse helped me back to bed. I started to come to terms with the extent of my injuries, along with the reality of my situation. I apologised to my mum and sister. I explained to them that I had no idea how bad I was until I saw myself in the mirror. I was discharged two weeks later to return home. Every bump on the car journey home, I could feel.

It felt like scissor ends jabbing into my back, while glass shards broke into smaller fragments under the skin. The intensity of this provoked physical detachment as a coping mechanism. It took all my strength, just to get home. I wasn't sure if I would get through this. A lot more strength was needed to cope with my pain. I finally reached a horizontal position. My bed, my room, and my possessions. The pain would flood through me in waves. I thought if the pain is going to be this bad I don't think I will make it. This thought was instantly changed by a radiating sense of peace. An orb of bright shining light appeared in the corner of the bedroom. A surge of energy radiated from my toes to my head. It took away all my pain. I felt so relieved. The orb faded and I was left with this new found peace. I had been shown a way through the pain. I stopped focussing on the pain and focussed on the memory of this feeling. I used this feeling memory to heal each broken bone and sore point within. I visualised and projected the orb of light into different parts of my body. This helped alleviate my pain and heal my broken bones. This became my ritual to handle what was going on. I also used herbal drops of Hypericum, Arnica and Comphrey. This was suggested by a naturopath friend of Kathy's. Each herbal remedy had effective healing attributes for my injuries. I had to wear a back brace whenever I wanted to get out of bed. I could not sit up for any longer than fifteen minutes at a time. I had a few friends come to visit not long after I returned home. They were so shocked to see me looking the way I did, they didn't come back again. Mum could only stay a month. Wayne was also going away for work. It was decided to organize the mobile nursing service to help me. The mobile nursing agency were booked to come twice a week on Tuesday and Friday. This was arranged by mum before she left. Mum and I had to improvise with the fact that I could not bend. I used a long stick with a protruding nail at one end, to help me pull up lower garments when dressing. Mum left on the Monday and did everything she could to make my life easier until the nurse came to visit the following day. Tuesday came around, but the mobile nursing service did not show up. I didn't know what to do. I decided to wait until Friday. Friday arrived and again no show of a nurse. I managed the best I could. I was starting to feel depressed.

It was hard, so hard to cope alone. I rang Wayne who was working away to ask him for help. He said all he could do was ring Kate's father to come and feed the horses. That afternoon a female friend Ruth called around, from my tertiary Fashion Design course. I was delighted to see her. She asked "who was looking after you". I replied "Me". I explained how the mobile nursing service had been booked to come and help me, but they didn't show up. Ruth said "Right pack your bags you are coming with me". I gasped and said "What do you mean". "You can't be here alone in your condition", Ruth said. I thanked her and asked her "Are you sure". Ruth insisted that it would be fine for me to stay with her. She said "I will not leave me you like this". Ruth had a spare room downstairs at her house, but no bed. She asked if I had a bed. I said "No". I assumed under the circumstances that Sven and Kate wouldn't mind if I borrowed the bed until I could get one of my own. Ruth arranged for the bed and my stuff to be picked up. I left a note, telling Kate and Sven of my new address, my health situation, and that I had borrowed the bed.

A week passed and I was rehabilitating slowly. The police showed up with a warrant to arrest me for theft and arson. I was in bed and I missed all the commotion. Ruth explained to the police that I had recently been involved in a severe car accident. She told them I was still recuperating and could not move unaided. Once the police knew about the car accident and my inability to move, they dropped the charges. They settled for the return of the bed. A few calls were made to local charity shops and we found another bed. They were kind enough to deliver the bed to us. Kate and Sven had returned home to find the room I had staying in guttered of its contents. Everything from the room was found on the back lawn burnt to a crisp. I was accused of stealing the bed and setting the contents of the room alight. I queried Wayne about this, as he knew the couple better than me. He was working away, and had no idea this had occurred. Still to this day I am perplexed as to who, why, and how this took place.

I carried on with my healing and pushed this horrible ordeal to the back of my mind. I did wonder why this car accident happened. I spent many horizontal hours researching the meaning of life, through a myriad of books. One book expressed that a car accident represented a crossroad in life. The path you were on needed to change abruptly. That it did. I recovered in half the time expected. After six months my broken bones knitted together.

This enabled me to start doing stretches to increase my physical strength. My spirit was empowered, by the deeper understanding I had achieved, of the bodies reaction to the mind. I listened to my physical limits, yet increased my visual desire to mend. I mentally fed myself encouragement, health, vitality, comfort, love, and all the key elements that assist in healing. Each day was a step closer to independence. When well enough I set foot into the world I once knew. Everything had changed, my goals, my outlook, and me.

Chapter 5

I found a share house close to the beach for only sixty dollars a week. It was with a thirty year old man named Richard. He was a good, all round descent bloke. We got along well. He introduced me to his alternative friends. He mentioned that a friend of his named Veronica was coming over the next day to give him a Reiki healing. He asked if I wanted one. I agreed, as it sounded interesting. It was something I had not tried before. Richard had his healing while I went for a walk to the beach. Veronica asked me to return in about an hour's time. When I arrived back Veronica asked me to lay her table and close my eyes. I just let whatever was going to happen, happen. I resonated with the feeling I felt from Veronica's hands as she scanned my body. It was similar to the healing I did with the bright orb on different areas of my body. I was very relaxed and felt the energy pass through the different areas. When the healing had finished, I was amazed how similar Reiki was to the healing I had done on myself. I explained this connection to her. I expressed my joy to know that I too could give this to others to help them heal. I inquired where she learnt Reiki and asserted myself to undertake the course. I was so happy to become aware of this being taught to others. I did my Reiki I, II, and III. This gave me the confidence to open up and share the innate healing abilities within me. Life had come full circle once again. I was beaming with delight at what the future had in store for me. My new flatmate Richard and I went out to night clubs every so often. This enabled me to meet other friends who also loved to dance.

I met a couple called Natasha and Ronald who hosted the best dance parties. I was invited to one of their gigs. It was up in the back blocks, on acreage. I was under the impression it was a rave party. A DJ friend of mine, Carl, was booked to do a set there. I got a lift with him and his mate

Sergio. It was summer and the rainy season. It rained all the way there, but stopped when we turned onto the dirt track leading to the property. There were quite a few cars parked on the open paddock. We proceeded to park adjacent to the other cars and became bogged in mud. It was only a small car, so the boys got out and tried to move it, to no avail. We decided to worry about it later. The music got louder as we made our way down the long drive. We saw Natasha and Ronald our mutual friends at the DJ booth. Looking around us we saw many faces we did not know. We felt out of place in comparison to them. We were dressed for a rave party. I wore silver flares and a rainbow coloured crop top. Carl wore a stark white track suit, and Sergio was in his designer dapper. All eyes were on us. The crowd was restless and uneasy. It looked more like a biker party to me. Everyone was dressed in dark clothes, flannelette shirts, and with hostile faces. We saw another mutual friend of ours Thomas. He had just finished playing a set at the party with his band. Thomas told us that it rocked, and expressed how the crowd loved it. Thomas said "The crowd were restless because the music had been changed to dance music". I replied "I thought this was going to be a rave party". Thomas said "No it's a guy's 50th that Natasha and Ronald know, he is part of the local biker gang". We approached Natasha and Ronald to ask what is going on. I asked if we were supposed to be here. They assured us that all would be fine. Ronald said "The guy who hired us doesn't mind dance music". "What about everyone else", I asked. They looked far from happy about it. Natasha said "Don't worry there is enough of us here to convert them through the music". I said "Are you kidding". I counted nine of us to about 150 of them, who were spread around 2 bonfires. There were even more people near a shed, that stood a few hundred metres away. The shed emanated a horrible feeling. Ronald said "Just fit in the best you can, they're not really that bad". I replied "Yeah it is alright for you having a black belt in Karate, we will be sticking by your side". Carl was carrying his box of records to the DJ booth and slipped over on the muddy ground, right under the stage lights. His white pants all covered in mud up one side. Carl quickly composed himself and was thankful his records stayed clean. Sergio and I tried to blend in to look as inconspicuous as possible, while Carl started playing his records. You could see the people around us looking at each other with arguable faces. I was feeling very uncomfortable and asked Sergio to hold my packet of cigarettes to free up my hands. Sergio tucked them under his T-shirt sleeve. We stood about five metres away from the stage. Ronald was next to us bopping his head to the music. Hay bales were set around the outskirts of the shed for seating. An unknown man approached Sergio and I. He stood right up close to our faces. He had a bottle of beer in his hand and asked us "What is this shit playing". He stated "This music only started when you guys turned up". I had a vision of this guy smashing the glass bottle over Sergio's head. The man was so angry at us. We played dumb and said we were invited by Natasha and Ronald. "Do you know Ronald?" I asked him. "No", he replied fiercely. I hoped Ronald would see us being hassled and come over to help. That didn't happen. The disgruntled man then asked for a smoke from Sergio. Sergio automatically replied that he doesn't smoke. He forgot that he had agreed to hold my packet of cigarettes. The man reached for Sergio's shoulder and grabbed at the cigarette packet saying "Well what are these then". The man then fell backwards over one of the hay bales. The man got up with the bottle still in his hand and said "I suppose you think that's funny". I think yes in my head, but I felt panicked in my body and replied "No". Sergio and I were as emotionally neutral as we could be. We made sure not to show any expression on our faces. The man just muttered under his breath and walked away. Sergio and I agreed, that was a narrow escape. People around us were getting more and more agitated, as Carl kept playing the dance music. Sergio and I approached Carl at the DJ booth. We gestured to him that we should go. Carl was annoyed at us because he was trying to mix songs. Carl pulled his headphones off one ear and said "WHAT". I said "Look around, everyone's so angry at the music you're playing, it is not safe here anymore". Natasha tried to reassure us saying "It's fine, we got death threats last time we did a party for them, but nothing happened, we will be ok as long as we all stick together". That was it. I lost it. I was trembling inside. I said "Are you crazy, there are nine of us and too many of them, we are leaving". Carl gives Sergio and me this funny look of realization that we are not safe. He starts to finish up his set. Sergio was getting pushy with Carl saying "Seriously, come on Carl". Natasha stepped in and took over the decks for Carl. This was not without a break in the music. The whole crowd loudly yelled their joy as the music ceased. Natasha started spinning her tracks once again. You could feel the crowds anguish propelled toward us like a choking fog. Sergio and I eagerly stood waiting while Carl packed up his records. I didn't even notice the other two people next to me, until I heard a woman's voice say my name. I looked over at this woman's eyes that were unfamiliar. I took at her face, her build, her hair. I was trying to piece together where she knew me from. I looked at her again and noticed the shape of her face. I did not recognize the eyes. That's not her eyes, I thought. They were so dark. It was Greta from the nursery cottage. The tarot card reader I had met many months earlier. Well that was it, I was spooked. If I could have run away I would have, but we had to stay together. I now hurried Carl by saying "Come on Carl, now". "Ok", Carl said disgruntledly. Carl reminded Sergio and me that the car was bogged. I wondered how we would get out of here. I see Thomas on the other side of the stage getting into a four-wheel drive. I hurry over to tell him Sergio, Carl and I have to go. I asked him if he could pull our car out of the bog at the top paddock. "Sure get in", he said. Sergio got in the back with the records. Carl and I got in the front. Thomas was oblivious to the escalating vibe of the party. He started telling us what a good deal he got for the car, and how he has wanted a 4wd for ages. Sergio then said "Their coming". Carl and I look out the back window to see five men approaching. They were walking from the shed. They were about thirty metres away, heading straight for the car. I tell Thomas to start the car as we need to go, now. Thomas turned the key, but the car doesn't start. Sergio then says "Their getting closer". Carl and I look behind us. Four more men have joined the first five. Carl asks Thomas what's was wrong with the car. Thomas replied "Nothing, it was going fine before". Thomas turned the key again but the car just coughs and splutters. Panicking for our lives I say to Carl "White light the engine, Sergio help us, we can do this focus". Sergio says "They are nearly here". At that moment the four-wheel drive kicks over and starts up. The three of us yell "Go, Go, Thomas, quick". Thomas was still unaware of the urgency. We make it out with only metres to spare. We watch the men lifting up their arms, yelling and ranting as we escape. "The people at the party were ok", Thomas said. "When our band were playing, they couldn't get enough". I informed Thomas that they hated the dance music Carl was playing. I said "They blamed us for it. The music changed when we got there. Thomas pulled our car out of the bog like a slippery bar of soap. Easy done. We were all overjoyed and couldn't thank Thomas enough. We felt indebted to him with our lives. The three of us tried to talk Thomas out of going back to the party.

Thomas was adamant all would be ok. I said "Ok it's your life". The three of us were too pumped with adrenalin from our timely escape to drive very far. We all agreed to get a safe distance away. Sergio said "There is a bridge about ten minutes away". "Ok let's go", Carl said. We didn't say much on the way to the bridge. There were a lot of sighs and positive verbal reinforcement like "we made it out". When we got to the bridge we were all flabbergasted. We shrieked out all the built up tension in emotional verbal accounts of what had just happened. Each one of us stating different and varied serial attacks by onlookers. Then there was Greta. I said "Carl, Greta was there, the tarot lady, I didn't even realize it was her because her eyes looked so dark, she was one of them". I thought of all those people that I sent to Greta who trusted her. "She has probably steered many of us off course and away from our destiny, or even driven us to our fate, oh my god, I can't believe it", I said.

Sergio said "We only just got out of there with our lives". Carl replied "I didn't realize it was that bad until Natasha told us about the death threats they got last time". Carl exclaimed how he also got a sinking feeling when the four-wheel drive wouldn't start. He said "You could feel the threatening energy coming closer and closer, I have never felt anything like it". Sergio asked "What were Natasha and Ronald thinking to invite us to such a dodgy party where our lives are in danger?" I replied "I don't know, but they have a lot to answer for". "Fancy trying to turn a pack of bikers into techno lovers overnight, you have got to be kidding", Carl said. "I have heard about music calming the savage beast but that was out of control", said Sergio.

The three of us gave Natasha and Ronald a wide berth until our emotions had settled. We felt we had not been given any warning or understanding as to what we were walking into that night. We buried the hatchet on the proviso we were given full details next time. Forewarned is forearmed.

A few months later Sergio and I attended another party that Natasha and Ronald hosted. This time it was at their home. The lounge room was converted to a dance floor. The lounges were placed outside in the back garden. The kitchen was turned into a DJ booth. It hosted two turntables and the most intense sound system. You couldn't help but move to the beat. The music went through you like wind pogo. Sergio and I were busting a move, and so was everyone else. My attention was drawn to a group of people in the middle of the room. One woman especially sparked my interest. She was dancing around a stunning looking girl. The more the woman danced around the girl, the more intense the woman's energy became. The woman then started to transform before my eyes. I saw her head lean back, with her jawline protrude forward. Her lips were slightly apart showing sharp teeth resembling a Jackal. I thought I was seeing things. I watched her snigger and jolt the top of her torso up and down, while circling this girl. I got close to Sergio to let him know what I had seen. Sergio asked "Which woman". I alerted his attention her way. Within moments of doing this the woman came dancing over to us. She was now back in human form. She danced between Sergio and me which created a repelling effect between Sergio and me. It felt like she was trying to push us apart. We just ignored her. She left and danced back to the original girl. I asked Sergio if he felt what the woman did. He said "Yes, you could feel her energy trying to separate us". I replied "She was trying to steal the energy between us Sergio". I felt uncomfortable with what had just happened, and also with what I had seen and felt. I decided to leave. I did make a point of visiting Natasha the next day to see who that woman was. I told Natasha that I saw the woman change into a Jackal and how I thought she was feeding off the energy of the girl. Natasha told me that the woman in question was named Ursula, and the girl she was dancing around was an international model. Natasha said "Ursula will be attending the big party coming up next month. Natasha suggested it would be a good opportunity to talk to her myself. I agreed. I thought of how I would approach someone I do not know and say "Hey I saw you turn into a Jackal at the last party". The turnout for the upcoming party was supposed to be huge, hosting a few hundred people. There was a ticket charge of thirty dollars. Natasha asked if I would like to work on the door for free entry to the event. I jumped at the chance, as the only other option was to help clean up after the event for free entry. The party theme was Africa. I covered white flares with black patches to resemble a Zebra and I made horns out of white felt pipe cleaners, as my outfit. It was cool working the door. It was a good way to meet those attending. I saw Ursula in the distance, making her way to the entrance. I thought now or never. I introduced myself and said "I noticed you at Natasha and Ronald's last party they had at their house. She seemed quite meek in her demeanour, and answered softly "Oh ok". I said "This is going to sound strange but the night of that party I saw you change into a Jackal looking creature". I said "It was only when you were dancing around that model". Ursula laughed and raised her head to look at me. She said "I don't get out much, so when I do, I let myself go". My reply was "I could see that". We gave each other the all-knowing look. I see you, and I you. It didn't sit well with me that I got no explanation from Ursula of what I witnessed. I thought it best I just steer clear of her. This was my first encounter with someone that could manipulate another person's energy. A modern day vampire.

Routine kicked in again. I attended work and my Fashion Design course. It was Mother's day morning the year 2000. I received a call that shook my foundations. Kathy rang to tell me our mum had passed away. I was in shock. I know you're supposed to cry, but how. This is not real, is it? I thought. Mum was my rock, my confidant, the one I would turn to when I needed to make sense of what was happening in my life. I am alone, so alone. The emptiness echoed through my chest, similar to the sensation of taking a deep breath in when sucking on a throat lozenge. Time had lost all meaning. The only importance now was the way I was feeling. I was not ready to lose my mother, I still felt so little and the world so big. The world was daunting without her. I could not go to work. I could not be around more than three or four people at the most. The thought of catching public transport was overwhelming. I just could not function without her. My sensitivity to others turned inward on myself. I was unaware of anything, except for the void within. I began drawing again. It was something I loved to do as a child. I was always good at copying other pictures for ideas or still life, but I never had the ability to draw from my imagination. After mums death something amazing happened. I was able to look at a blank piece of paper and a face would appear to me on the page. I would then proceed to outline the face with sticks of coloured chalk. The chalks were a gift from my mother many years ago. This ability went on for days and months, as I proceeded through my grief and loss. It seemed like some kind of healing therapy. This ability became second nature for me. My friends would ask who the people were that I was drawing. I could not tell them. The faces just appeared on the page. My good friend Sally told me of a lady she once saw at a spiritual fair that did similar drawings to my own. Sally went on to tell me that this lady called her pictures "Spirit guide drawings". Sally asked what I did to make the faces appear. I had to think about this as I never really took any notice, it just happened. I realized that it occurred when I connected to my heart. Sally asked "Have you ever tried to connect to anyone else. "No", I replied. Sally asked me if I wanted to try and connect to her. I said "Sure, let's try". I asked Sally to put her hands on the table, and I put mine on top of hers. I closed my eyes and opened my heart to connect with hers energetically. Images started flooding in, it was a like a conga line of people wanting to have their picture drawn. I broke my hands free of Sally's and started to draw the first face I had seen. It was a boy, a teenage boy. The more I drew the clearer he became. I gained an understanding of his character and certain signature gestures, like his walk. I could feel him emotionally and what he wanted to communicate. This led me to describe to Sally what I was feeling as I drew this boy. When I had finished the picture, I turned it around to show Sally. Sally's eyes welled up with tears. She said "I know who that is". "Do you recognize him", I questioned. Sally said "When you described his walk I knew who it was". I felt for Sally as I could see this was bringing up sad emotions. I asked Sally if she was alright. Sally said "Yes, thank you, it is good to know he is ok". I said "Who is it may I ask". Sally told me it was her eldest brother who had committed suicide when she was young. I gave her my heart-felt apologies for her loss. I had only known Sally a few short years. Sally said "What you have is a gift". I thanked Sally for showing me what I can do with this gift. I practised on other people that I trusted and found out these pictures can also be related to those close to our hearts in the past, present or the future. Sometimes the face was not familiar to people, but the characteristics made a connection. It was a way to step outside of my own feelings and connect back to others. This in part helped bring me back emotionally.

Chapter 6

A few months passed before my next vision. I was shown a natural disaster which was going to flood most of Australia. The same male voice I had heard from my first vision said that the top end of Australia was going to be the safest and highest plateau to avoid this tragedy. My feelings turned toward the future, knowing I had to get there.

After almost a decade up north, where circumstance led to self-healing and transformation, I became clearer. I trusted my intuition like never before. I was now able to view that within and around me with truth.

I received an insurance pay out from the car accident that I had endured 3 years earlier. This enabled me to set up a new life. To my surprise my sister Kathy had moved to the same area where I was drawn to live, only 6 months earlier with her young daughter.

I was happy to know I had a connection there and that I would not be completely on my own.

I stayed with my sister Kathy until I found my own place to live. It was great to see her and my niece Elexis again after so many years apart. Kathy had lived down south for the past decade which meant we seldom made the trek interstate to visit each other. It was a week before the Melbourne Cup, so we decided to attend a luncheon at the local hotel in honour of us connecting again. It was great fun getting all dolled up and chatting about the years gone by. We interjected at how mum's death had shaken us both. The year after her loss was like a blur. Nothing of importance was noted, we just existed.

Kathy and I regained our close bond once more. One evening out of the blue Kathy started telling me of the round purple rug she had in her room. Kathy went on to tell me that at night she would be visited by spirits. She would then suddenly be on the rug. The spirits talked to her and showed her pictures on a screen, similar to a movie. I was nearly bursting to tell her my account of the purple rug too. I knew if I did, that it would interfere with what she was to convey. Kathy explained that she would pretend to be asleep, and shallow breathe, in the hope they would leave. The rug seemed to be floating above darkness. Kathy would then wake up on the rug, alone and jump from the rug to her bed. She was scared that the floor was going to disappear from under her. I eagerly said "Kathy the same thing used to happen to me when I was little, what a relief I am not crazy after all", I laughed. I told her of my childhood experiences with the round purple rug, which were the same as hers. We then wondered where the purple rug come from and how long it had been in the family. Did our eldest sister Patricia have the rug in her room too? Did she also get visited at night by spirits? Mum was not around to ask anymore and our sister Patricia was scared of anything to do with the supernatural. We decided to ask her one day, but the right time has not arisen to do so yet.

I was still working through the grief from the loss of my mother. I started questioning whether this was normal, considering it was now over a year since her passing. I saw an advertisement for a twelve week counselling course in the local paper. It started at the end of the month. I decided to enrol. I figured this would help me understand where I am at within myself, and as to whether I was doing ok. It was quite daunting at first meeting so many new people. It was good to find out the agenda's everyone had for joining the course. Many had chosen this course to find direction within their lives, and seek some form of confirmation on how to deal with these issues. One part of the course worked through reflective listening. This highlighted to me, how well I was able to tune into others, even though my own grief felt like it filled much of my being. I was relieved I could still do this. I wanted to claim my life back and the ability to care outside of my own emotional state. We were also introduced to a list of stages relating to death and dying. The emotional steps could be experienced in any order and re-experienced within the grieving process for as long as two to three years. The counsellor stated that by after the third year if little improvement, emotional growth or understanding was gained by the individual, that they may need to seek professional counselling. I was doing ok. I was normal. I was working through what I was feeling and proud to be doing the right thing by myself. I gained my certificate 1 in basic counselling skills. I felt more together and able to take the next step in my life.

This led me to research my interest in Iridology (diagnosis of the eyes). I could not shake the image of when I first saw my eyes in the mirror at the hospital, after the car accident. They looked like a marble print of purple, blue and red in the whites of the eye. I had small dark spots within the iris. Through my interest and research I found an accredited correspondence course in Iridology. This course was part of an advanced diploma of Naturopathy. I underwent the study and found that our eyes reflect our internal state through them. If we break a bone, this will reflect in the corresponding body zone of the iris as a black lesion or spot. If the bone heals, the black lesion or spot subsides with the healing. This is exactly what happened with my eyes. Day by day they would change as my body repaired itself. I was so enthralled with the information learnt, that I passed with a high distinction. This was great, but to work within the industry I needed a certain amount of practical work experience. This experience included using an iridology camera. I rang all the local Naturopaths to seek experience, yet no one would take me on. I took this as a sign that my work was done. I had achieved great marks in my course and learnt what I needed to know to satisfy my curiosity in this field.

Chapter 7

I now felt strong enough to go it alone and find my own space. I found a lovely little house to rent on a quarter acre block. It was central to the city and the beach, being only twenty minutes away from each in opposite directions. I was looking through the paper and saw an advertisement reading red cloud puppies for sale. I had an affinity with this breed after spending my school holidays on my sister Patricia's farm with their red cloud dog. I rang the number and set up a time to view the puppies. I was taken by the absolute cuteness of the six puppies and wondered how I would choose. One of the puppies came and sat at my feet. He looked up at me as if to say "pick me". I was in love with this chocolate brown bundle of joy who I named Rusty. There was a local park a few minutes' walk from my house. I took Rusty there every afternoon for a run. There I met a wonderful array of dog owners that also frequented the park every afternoon. Rusty made some good friends and so did I. This is where I met my dear friend Justine. Justine owned a large dog that was her baby and protector. She was a very gentle lady, who never spoke out of turn about anything or anyone. I found it very easy to talk and confide in her. This led me to find out that she also did healings. We arranged to give each other a healing on a weekly basis. This interaction propelled my confidence and understanding of my gifts. I became more in tune with my healing vibration and the positive effect it had on others. Justine was twice my age and through her experience she became a spiritual mentor for me. I learnt about spiritual boundaries, grounding techniques, lucid dreaming, and intuitive writing to name but a few. This opened a deeper connection to myself and my inner-knowing. I was starting to see the bigger picture of how my life's experiences thus far, had shaped my future.

Justine asked if I wanted to meet her friend Tina. Tina was also a healer. I agreed. Justine asked if I would like a healing from them both on the day. I accepted the offer as I had never had a healing done by two people before. Tina was lovely and very welcoming. I was shown to a room with a massage table and asked to lay down. Justine was at my feet and Tina at my head. I relaxed and closed my eyes. Healings are a wonderful way to relax the mind, body, and spirit. Justine asked if I saw or felt a colour. I said "Yes yellow". Justine went on to say "We now surround you in the colour yellow, penetrating, healing, and invigorating every cell of your being in yellow, supporting, comforting, nurturing and grounding you're physical, cellular, etheric, and magnetic bodies in the colour yellow". The gap between her last words and my body's reaction seemed like only a few moments. My whole body started convulsing, from my head to my toes. A voice came through me from deep in my chest saying calmly "It is amazing what the body remembers, this is the physical trauma from my car accident coming out". Justine asked "Are you ok". I replied "Yes, I am not scared, it needs to come out". "Good", Justine said. I could still feel Tina holding my head and Justine holding my feet. I am not sure how long the convulsions lasted. I was experiencing what was happening from a different level of consciousness. It was like a dream that I was awake in. The convulsing subsided to a mild shiver. Justine and Tina asked how I was. "Tired", I said. Justine said that I had shifted a lot in the one session and that it best I rest now. Justine made me comfortable by placing a blanket over me and a pillow to cuddle. I felt washed out, but very relaxed. I couldn't believe what had just happened. I had all that inside of me. I felt so much lighter. I thanked them both for their help. Justine said "You were ready to let it go, we just kept you grounded during the process".

It was nearing two years now, since mum had passed away, but I still missed her greatly. I would often chat to her in my quiet time, asking for resolve in different situations of my life. I could still feel our mother/daughter connection strongly within myself. I would resolve my issues by questioning what Mum would say. By doing this I realized all the wonderful self-resilience and ability she had instilled within my character. Mum wasn't that far from me after all. She was in my problem solving, my understanding, my heart, and my life. The only thing missing was her physical body. Mum was right here, I could feel her as though she was standing next to me. It dawned on me that I was holding her here. She was unable to pass over until she knew I was going to be ok. I had to come to terms with my grief and my unwillingness to let her go. This needed to be done so both her and I could move on. I shut my eyes and told her I would be ok now, you can go. I felt mum's peaceful relief. I witnessed her physical image being pulled like a vacuum, shrinking into the distance, becoming a tiny dot of light, then vanishing. I opened my eyes. I felt good about myself. I was finally able to let her go. Pivotal times in my life when I really did need her comfort, she would return, in my dreams to give me a cuddle. The distance between our world and the dearly departed is lessened by the hearts connection.

A short time passed before I met with Justine again. She told me of a self-help cancer clinic that were looking for healers to do volunteer work with their patients. I expressed that I am not sure if I am ready to work with the public. Justine said "You are ready, it is natural to feel a bit anxious". We attended an interview with the presiding Doctor. Justine and I were asked to attend the clinic the following Monday at 5.30. We were asked to attend the support group meeting after our healing work. The nutritionist doctor and her psychologist husband ran the clinic. They were both convinced that alternative healing modalities had a place beside modern medicine. It was great working with such open minded professionals. Each Monday a guest speaker would attend the support group meetings. There was a wonderful array of teachings each week conveyed from a sound therapist, cranial-sacral therapist, polarity therapist chromo-therapy (colour therapy), and more. We also learnt breathing techniques, visualisation techniques, and how thoughts can affect our emotions as researched by Masaru Emoto with water crystals. There was also new scientific evidence discussed concerning herbal/nutritional breakthroughs in the fight against cancer. I was proud to help others in such a delicate time of their lives. I arrived early one Monday evening. I decided to wait out the front in my car until it was time to go in. It was on dusk and a car pulled up, facing towards me. The driver was a mature lady, who emanated a peaceful warm glow. I hadn't even met her yet, but I could feel how nice she was. She got out of the car, wearing a lovely purple shawl. She looked over at me and smiled with a genuine heart-warming smile. I smiled back, with happiness inside. What a beautiful lady, I thought to myself. I collected my massage table and linen to make my way into the healing rooms. I finished the healing session then joined the group *upstairs for the support meeting. To my surprise the lady I had noted out front with the purple shawl was the guest speaker of the night. Her name was Mary, she was a psychologist/psychotherapist who used meditation within her practice. Mary was in remission from cancer. She expressed personally, what helped her come to terms with the condition. Art therapy played a big part in connecting to and understanding her Cancer. She took us all through a guided meditation, which was delightfully relaxing & refreshing. Mary then announced that she held a meditation group or Satang at her home twice a week. I approached her after the meeting and couldn't help but imply how she radiated warmth. Mary said "Takes one to see one". We smiled. I enquired about her meditation classes and decided to attend that coming Saturday. I was interested in what sort of people would attend. I got there to find a differing array of characters and ages. Our shoes were taken off outside the front door. Mary greeted each of us personally, one by one, before we could enter the room. She would look deep into your eyes as if checking your soul's demeanour. She would then withdraw her intent gaze and invite you in, with a gentle warm smile. The front room of her home had a lounge suite and chairs set up in a semi-circle. Big bay windows gave a sense of openness and space. There were twelve people that attended the class that day. We all found a chair, with Mary seated on one side, facing toward the group. She asked us to close our eyes and take a few deep breathes. This was the first time I had meditated. I was anxious and wondering if everyone really did have their eyes closed. I had a quick peek. Yes they all did, so I then felt I could relax. Well I tried to relax. My mind nattering all different aspects of the vulnerable situation I found myself in, with strangers surrounding me. Mary started to speak in a calm tone. She spoke of varying analogies of stillness and the ability to let things pass, to not hold any thought, just let it pass. One analogy she used was of clouds. She explained that underneath the clouds there is always a constant blue sky, never changing regardless of the stormy clouds in front of it. Our aim was to be that blue sky. To go beyond the clouds and reveal our constant, unwavering selves. This part of us would not be moved by stormy skies. I felt like I had dropped my awareness. Like a haze, a vision appeared. It was my face screaming. This scene propelled me back. I sat, still with my eyes closed, wondering what the hell that was. "It was me", I replied to myself. Why am*

I screaming, I thought. I decided not to pressure on myself as it was the first time I had meditated. I was probably scared.

Mary brought our awareness back, by asking us to wriggle our toes, our fingers, and to become aware of our body. We were asked to open our eyes when ready. Mary asked us not to look at each other. She asked that we just sit with how we feel and asked if anyone wanted to share how they were feeling. An older man of the group started to speak. He told us that when he relaxed deeply emotional pain arose. Mary asked the man "Can you feel the emotional pain now". The man said "Yes". Mary asked him to close his eyes and connect with the feeling of pain. The man said "I am too scared in case the feeling engulfs me". Mary said "Once you have connected to this pain completely it will change". She explained "This feeling has risen to the surface to be noticed, and your awareness needs to acknowledge and understand why you have this feeling, in order for you to then, be able to let it go". Mary said "I will support you through the process". Mary again asked him to connect to the pain he felt. She asked him to describe what it looked like. The man said "It is dark and murky". Mary asked if he could drop into the dark murkiness and really feel it within. The man agreed. A couple of minutes passed and then Mary asked how the man was feeling. The man said "My first image of the dark murkiness was clearing". She asked him to stay with the image and feeling. The man opened up and shared what incident sparked this pain. Mary asked "Is this pain in the past or present". The man replied "The past". She asked him why he was still carrying past hurt. The man said "Because I could not forgive myself". Mary asked "Can you forgive yourself now, that you have seen what it looks like inside of you". The man said "Yes, I am willing to let it go". Moments later the man's voice changed. He sounded brighter. The man said "The dark, murkiness is clearing". Mary asked "What do you see now". The man replied "There are colours, bright colours flashing in my eyes". Mary asked how he was feeling. The man said "Happier, now I have faced what I have done". Mary complimented the man on his courage. She asked if anyone else would like to share. A woman piped up and said that she too had the same issue of forgiveness from her past. She said "Hearing the man work through his own story also helped her to let go". This was reiterated by verbal acknowledgement from a few others in the group. Mary adjourned the group and asked us to help ourselves to refreshments in the next room. I was in awe at the peace coming through this man's face. He looked years younger than when he arrived. I didn't stay for a cuppa because I was overwhelmed by what I had just witnessed. I thanked Mary for the opportunity to be involved in such a wonderful and caring group. She asked if I would be coming back next week. I said "Yes". I said goodbye to everyone and said how nice it was to meet them.

My sister Kathy lived only five minutes down the road. I decided to pop in and tell her about the meditation group. My sis made me a cuppa and I proceeded to tell her about the man in the group. My sister asked how I found out about the group. I explained to her that I met Mary as a guest speaker at the cancer clinic where I did volunteer work. I told her the story of how Mary pulled up in the car opposite me and how she radiated warmth. I told Kathy that she wore a lovely purple shawl. Kathy replied "That is the same way you described the woman who helped bring you back to life, when you came out of a coma". I said "I don't remember that, remind me". Kathy said "You spoke of two older ladies that helped bring you back to life, one of them was wearing a purple shawl, you kept talking about the purple shawl, and how the women radiated with light". I replied "That is bizarre, it was Mary, and it had to be". "Who was the other lady", I asked. Kathy said "You didn't describe her as much as the one with the purple shawl, you said they comforted you and brought you back to life". "Wow, life is amazing", I said. I thanked sis for reminding me of this.

I attended the next meditation class with Mary the following week. I was a little more relaxed this time, considering I had already met most of the people in the group the previous week.

We sat with our eyes closed as Mary delivered yet another beautiful imagery meditation on releasing our truth. I felt myself slip into a subliminal state. I felt like I was almost asleep, but conscious of my surroundings. Images started to appear in my mind of my prevailing dreams. These dreams related to people I had come into contact with. They were usually people I knew, who seemed to have another side to them. I would see the other side of them portrayed in dreams as a negative entity. This entity persuaded them to do atrocious things. I would bear witness to these incidents, hiding in the background. I was scared to be there. In some instances I would be seen by the entity, who would then make a point of trying to scare, imprison, or capture me. I became a victim to these nightmares. I did not want to fall sleep for fear of what would come to me in my dreams. We finished the meditation and Mary asked if anyone wanted to share how they felt. I plucked up the courage to talk of the screaming face I saw the week prior. Mary asked me to connect to that face, with my eyes closed. I did. My chest tightened. Mary asked how I was feeling. I said "Scared. She assured me that I was safe and she would be there to guide me. She asked if I could stay with this feeling, as uncomfortable as it seems. I said "I will". The screaming girl faded and I saw my body on the ground. I was reliving the car accident, after impact. I told Mary as it was happening. I was witnessing everything from outside my body. I was my soul. I saw a large group of people walking in the same direction. I wanted to follow them. There was such a strong sense of belonging. I couldn't leave to follow them I was stuck. Mary asked me to scan my body and see where I was stuck. I did this. I saw my soul had risen out of my body, with only its feet anchored into my chest. Mary asked if I could call the soul back into my body. I replied "I am not sure". She asked me to talk to my soul, to let it know that I had survived the car accident and that it doesn't need to leave my body. I did this in my own words as Mary was being my directive. My soul drew back into my physical body. Mary asked me how I felt. I said "I feel full again, I want to jump and wiggle, in what feels like my new body". Mary said "Well do it". I jumped up and opened my eyes then shook my limbs with a smile. "I am back", I said. I realised I had been stuck between two worlds. My soul was ready to leave my body due to the intense trauma of the car accident. Mary and the group were very happy for me. They noted the warmth I now reflected. I asked Mary whether this would stop the nightmares I had been having since the car accident. Mary replied "I am not sure". I was so happy. I convinced myself that the nightmares would stop, because I was no longer linked to the after world. Scientific research has been documented on OBE's (out of body experiences) incurred after varying traumatic experiences, where the soul leaves the body for self-preservation. The soul then returns after the trauma has passed. Some researchers state that this is a defence mechanism to deal with the threat of death.

I felt invigorated, open and carefree after this experience. I was lighter in spirit, than I had been in years. I took my evening stroll to the park with my dog Rusty. We were both elated to enjoy the fresh air. I noticed Justine sitting slumped over. She was not looking good. I asked if she was ok. Justine said she was not handling life very well at the moment. Before I could reply, Justine started to have a panic attack. Luckily another spiritual lady named Dot was there. She knew what to do. Dot asked Justine to tap on her thymus gland (2 fingers down from throat hollow) to calm herself and focus on taking deep breaths. Justine resumed her calm composure after about five minutes. I was concerned for her well-being as I had never seen her so vulnerable. Justine decided to make her way home. I asked if she would be ok. Justine said "Yes, but can I see you tomorrow for a healing". "Of course", I replied. Justine arrived at my house the next morning, looking as white as a ghost. I asked her what was going on with her. Justine told me that she was having reoccurring nightmares from her past. I asked what about. She told me about a man she had dated a few years back. He had abused her. Justine had tried to forget about it and move on, but the guilt and pain ran deep for her. I got Justine a glass of water and asked her to come outside to sit down in the fresh air. Justine said she really needed a healing. I said close your eyes and try to relax. I put my hands on either side of her head. I could feel the vibrations of her mind whizzing and darting under my palms. I made sure to ground myself. I found the longer my hands stayed on her head the slower the pulsing became. I was able to ease the whirring thoughts. The imagery I got from holding her head were like two horizontal cogs. The top one was spinning at a rapid pace, while the one underneath was moving at the pace of a second hand on a clock. Eventually the top cog slowed down enough to slot back into the lower cog. The erratic thought patterns had ceased and a sense of balance was regained. I asked Justine how she felt. Justine said "A lot calmer, thank you". I asked her to write down all that was troubling her, to get it out and then burn the piece of paper. Justine said she could feel her head starting to whirr again. I asked whether she was going to be ok. Justine said she will do the writing and then see how she feels. I offered my support to her if she needed anything. Justine had only been gone a few hours when there was a knock at the door. It was Dot, our other friend from the park. Dot informed me that she had just come from seeing Justine. I asked how she was. Dot said that Justine was having suicidal thoughts. Both Dot and I decided we would keep an eye on her, by checking alternate times during the day and evening. The next morning I arrived at Justine's to find Dot already there. Dot told me that the house seemed empty. This concerned both of us. We checked the outskirts of the house, yelling out to Justine and knocking on the windows and doors. Eventually we heard a noise from inside, then the front door opened. Justine looked drained. She had taken a sleeping pill to knock her out, and as a result she found it hard to wake up. Dot and I were relieved Justine was alive. Justine said she would like to get herself showered and dressed. She asked if Dot and I could call back in an hour. Dot and I left talking of how relieved we were that Justine was still with us. We both agreed how worrying this situation was. We were both concerned that she was there all night alone. When we returned to Justine's she had a bag packed. Justine said "I have booked myself into the local psychiatric centre for professional help. We agreed that would be best. Justine's daughter came to pick her up and drove her to the centre. I visited Justine every day. The first week was a bit unsettling for Justine, as she had only seen nurses to administer medication. She said that the medicine made her feel numb and drowsy. Justine was still herself but at a much slower rate of self-expression. The first week was all about getting her medication to manageable levels. Justine confided in me that she had not seen a therapist to talk through the issues troubling her. Three more days passed. Still no one took the time to get to the root of Justine's problem, which had resulted in her crisis. When Justine questioned the nurse as to when she would be seen by a therapist, the nurse responded by questioning whether the medication was stopping the suicidal thoughts. When Justine agreed the medication was helping, the nurse told her that she would not need a therapist because the medication is working well for her. Justine decided to sign herself out after two weeks. She was asked to keep taking the anti-depressants and if told she had any further problems to come back so they could adjust the dosage. It pains me to say but something was lost in Justine from that time. The anti-depressants dulled her spirit. They only put a band-aide on a wound that remains unhealed.

I had the privilege in my travels of befriending an ex-psychiatric nurse, Beatrice. She worked as a psyche nurse in the 1970's. Psychiatric care was handled very differently then. Anti-depressants were only given in the short term, until the individual had enough emotional separation from their presiding issue to gain strength. While attending therapy classes they would be taught problem solving skills to deal with their emotions. This enabled patients to come up with their own solutions. The medication was used as a stepping stone, until the person had gained a healthy sense of how to deal with the issue and heal themselves. Today these medications are used to blot the problems out. This prevents us from facing our emotional weaknesses. By facing our emotional weakness with proper support, we gain self-worth and inner-strength to overcome our crisis.

Justine decided to sell her house and move closer to her daughter. I missed her friendship and kindness immensely. Justine pointed out that it was now my time to grow. I needed to be in charge of my life and use what I had learned, or as Justine put it, what I remembered. This was so true, I had been shown the tools to do the work needed, to affectionately make a close bond with my inner- self. The part of us that knows.

I attended the next Satang meditation at Mary's. It had become a routine for me. I had worked through so much, and I felt a lot lighter because of it. The group consisted of a rag tag bunch who saw, understood, and supported each other. It was freeing to be surrounded by real people, who did not wear masks to camouflage their true selves. At the end of the Sat sang meditation Mary announced that her Cancer had returned and she was becoming progressively unwell. She was not sure if her health would hold out to take any more classes. We were all shocked. We were all honourable in our concern for this openly, caring woman who had helped change our lives. A short time later I was contacted to attend Mary's funeral. This was the first funeral I had been to. I arrived to see familiar faces and a wonderful array of different people. They ranged from business professionals to hippies, eccentric arty types, young families, teenagers. All walks of life together to join in the celebration of this beautiful woman's life. I heard lots of different stories telling how these people had met Mary. The crux of their meeting was always her valued truth, integrity and caring nature. I picked a red rose from my garden to lay on her coffin. The time came to approach the coffin and pay our respects. A big wave of emotion rose from my belly to my eyes. I rested the rose on her coffin. I thanked her for all she had done for me. I walked back to the pew with a lightened sense of will, knowing she was at peace. We all sat down once again. I watched Mary's coffin slowly lower into the cavity below her. At that very moment, I witnessed a wisp of black smoke gain volume and density, then suck upwards towards the roof, then disappear. A lady at the front row, who I had never seen before, turned and looked me straight in the eye, right after this had happened. It was the look of knowing between us. Mary's spirit had departed before our eyes. I left the service with such reverence and joy to have been a part of her life. How blessed I was to see with these eyes and feel with this heart. As I neared my car, I heard a guitar playing and a man singing. I drew closer to the noise and spotted the van he was in. The door was open and a clear, fresh spirited man sat enjoying his music. I asked whether he had been to Mary's funeral. He said "Yes, I used to play the guitar after her Sat sang meditations", but I hadn't been for a while". He was not sad about this, but joyous for her life and the time he spent with her. I agreed and said Mary is a part of everything now. The wind in the trees, the clouds in the sky, everything, every cell now one with nature. We smiled at each other and I went on my way.

Chapter 8

I have always been fascinated with varying types of attitudes and behaviours in people. This interest led me to apply for a position as a Carer. I put all my energy into my work as a Carer to obtain my certificate three in home and community care. Within my job I visited eight clients daily that needed personal assistance in their homes. My clients consisted of the convalescing, elderly, or the mildly disabled. I got to know each client closely. Over time I got to know their needs, wants, dreams, fears, and troubles. The job role was so varied for each client. Bonds of trust and integrity were formed, but with one woman more than any other. Mrs Tyrone was a ninety six year old lady born in 1901. I visited her five mornings a week to assist with daily routines. to start the day. Dementia had played havoc on her short term memory, which prevented her from knowing what she had done only moments before. My job was to assist her with showering, dressing, and personal hygiene. Her mind was as sharp as a tack when it came to remembering her childhood years. I heard many a story, more than once, which really alerted me to what was important in her life. Dementia has a way of burning out fuses of memory, sometimes forever and other times re-building pathways of the mind to reveal a lucid, clear individual. This type of fluctuation happened often to Mrs Tyrone. I witnessed a remarkable knowing with her ability to remember emotionally poignant times in her life, not with her memory but with her heart.

On more than one occasion she said "There is something special about today but I can't remember". I would pass this information onto her daughter Catherine, who would be able to pinpoint the exact emotional memory to her mother. It was beautiful, but also sad. Painful memories would also surface, like the death of a loved one. As you can imagine this memory was felt like the day it happened for Mrs Tyrone due to her failing memory. Mrs Tyrone would ask repeatedly ask me "Why am I still here". My reply was "You must have something important left to do". There were a few times I thought we were going to lose her. Some days she was so frail that she found it hard to raise an arm let alone her eye lids. Dignity is so important for anyone in this situation. Don't think for a minute that because someone is losing their memory that they are also losing feeling. Just when you'd accept her demise and say good bye, Mrs Tyrone would be sitting up in bed the next day pleased to see you. "Oh dear did you have a nice holiday", was one of the responses to seeing me. I was always honest with a bit of humour I replied "I was right here waiting for you to wake up, you have been sick and catching up on beauty sleep". She would then query me and ask how long she was sick. She would then apologise for any trouble she may have caused. She was never any trouble.

That was the first time I heard her account of what happened when she was so frail and couldn't wake. She told me of two men outside her window. "Yes", was my reply thinking she must of been hallucinating. I asked if she felt unsafe. "No", she said "They have visited me before". I asked if she knew them. She said "I know who they are, one is a doctor and the other one is like an angel". Mrs Tyrone asked me not to tell her daughter incase she thought she was going crazy. "I won't, I said "I am interested in your story". Mrs Tyrone said "You probably think I am crazy". I replied "No I don't actually, because there are lots of things in this world that can't be explained, that does not mean that they are not real". She smiled. "So what did they want", I asked. She went on to tell me that one came in to examine her. "Examine" I ask questionably. "Yes like a check-up", she said. "Oh ok", I replied and nod. "Go on", I said. "As he checks me over he reports to the other man outside the window how I am physically". "Gee that is amazing", I reply. "It sounds like they are helping to keep you alive", I said. Mrs Tyrone replied "I don't know why for a silly old duck like me". I again reiterate "You must have something important left to do". She smiles and thanked me for what I said. "I love hearing your stories they are interesting", I said. I thought to myself afterwards, gee that was one for the books. It was such an unusual story, that it has stuck with me. Months passed and again we were faced with the fact we might lose Mrs Tyrone. This turn lasted over a week. Once again she defied death and came back to us. It took a couple of days to bring her round properly into the land of the living. I managed to get her back into routine and share some laughs. She would often get flabbergasted with herself when she couldn't remember what she had done moments earlier, amidst her morning routines. She would question me in regards to what step she was up to. She would say "You must think I am silly". I replied "No, if you think of how many times you have done that task in 99 years, it is not very important in comparison to significant times in your life". This conversation provoked her to tell me of this weird dream she had. She told me that she noticed two men at her bedside. I asked "Did you know who they were". "I am not sure, but they felt familiar", she replied. I thought because she was under the weather and a bit spacey it may have been her Grandson and Son in law. I asked if she could describe them. She said "Not really, but they were nice to me, they came to give me a check-up and an injection". I was puzzled. "An injection", I questioned. "Yes, I felt better after the injection, I am sure he was my doctor", she said. I told Mrs Tyrone how worried we all were when she was sick. Her daughter then walked into the room. I asked her daughter if there their doctor had come to see her mum when sick. She said "Yes". I went on to ask "And did the Doctor give her an injection". "No", was her reply. "Oh ok I was just checking as your mum recalls the doctor giving her an injection". Her daughter said "The doctor took her pulse and temperature but that was all, he said we will have to wait and see".

Later on that morning I asked Mrs Tyrone about the doctor who came to see her when she was sick. "Was I sick", she asked. "Yes and we thought you were not coming back this time", I replied. I asked her about the two men she told me about that came to visit her. "Oh them, they have been coming more often now, I still don't know their names, isn't that silly", she says. "No, it sounds like they are too busy checking you over and making sure you are ok", I said. I asked her "Is the doctor the same one who visited with the other man you called an angel". Mrs Tyrone looked startled. "How do you know about them", she asked. "You told me the story last time you were sick, it is ok I believe you", I said. "Good because a lot of people would think I am going crazy", she said. "Not me, I believe in lots of things other people can't see", I said. She gives me a smile and said "Thank you".

In time I noticed Mrs Tyrone had a slight disregard for some men. It was like something had happened to her which affected her trust and ability to get along with them. A real lack of respect. I tried to help find its source through her stories, in the hope of putting it to rest. The aggravation spanned many years from her early childhood. She was the only girl in the family of five boys. She was expected to cook and clean up after them. She wanted to rough house and play as much as her brothers, but her household chores took up any of her play time. She loved horses and told me many stories about going to school on a horse and buggy. Mrs Tyrone became a professional woman as soon as she was old enough to leave home. She worked as a secretary, where she was able to finally be in charge of her own life. She married late in her years due to the fact of not wanting the job of cook, cleaner, and minder like that of her childhood. She got a lot off her chest in sharing her stories with me. Mrs Tyrone was able to forgive the past and lift the weight from her life's story. She finally found peace nearing the end of her 99 years in this world.

I am not a qualified consultant on Dementia but from my observations of this illness, it appears to block pathways of memory we cannot, or do not wish to remember or deal with anymore. Peace of mind comes from letting go. Mrs Tyrone was the last client in my work as a carer.

Chapter 9

I took a well-earned holiday to visit a dear friend of mine Soluntra and her four year old daughter Karey. I was warmed to hear that Karey imagined that I lived in a tree outside in their backyard. This helped Karey feel closer to me when I moved away. Karey told me that faeries live in the tree too. I asked her which tree. She took me outside and showed me a young eucalyptus tree. She said "This was how I would talk to you". How beautiful, I thought. I told Karey how much I missed her too.

We went back inside and sat on the lounge facing two roof to floor, double glass windows. We had a view out onto the backyard. Karey and I started talking. I noticed a small hazy figure about 20cm in height. It was standing on the ground, just outside the window looking in. I focused on the figure to see an outline of a tiny girl with wings, static, and pulsating in and out of focus. I alerted Karey to the figure. I asked "Is that one of them". She said "Yes". Then followed by a giggle. As soon as we both acknowledged the figure it zipped off. It left a blur of static energy behind. It was similar to the snowstorm effect on a television between channels, only in the shape of a faerie. I said to Karey "Gee their quick aren't they". Karey replied "Yes", with a big smile.

We are only limited by our imagination. I swore that after my car accident I would no longer question what I saw and felt. To look at the world with childlike eyes can open you up to magical experiences.

Chapter 10

I return home. Life is good. I have my own house, chooks, fruit trees in the backyard, and my dog Rusty. I gained my certificate three in home and community care. Yet something stirred inside of me.

I was in bed, almost asleep. I felt a finger prod me on my temple. I acknowledge this, but I don't think too much about it and fall asleep. I become increasingly uneasy each day after that night. I got stomach cramps. They came and went sporadically, without warning. I feel well other than this, in fact my mind and spirit haven't felt stronger. This fact distressed me. I wondered what was going on. I lived as normal until the cramps start to inhibit my way of life.

I confide in my trusted spiritual friend Justine on what has occurred. She advised me to meditate on the area where I was experiencing these cramps to see what comes up. She advised to do this every day for seven days. I did this and found as the day's progressed, I was getting more clues. This unrest does not belong to me, well not anymore as I found out.

The meditations took me back to my childhood, where I would have my teddy's and dolls packed shoulder to shoulder protecting me from the beings that would wake me in the night. I used to shallow breathe in the hope they thought I was asleep and leave. They never did. I recall sitting on the round purple rug in my room surrounded by beings. They showed me pictures on a screen that sat above me. I saw myself through the years on this screen. As I grew there was always a boy that was with me on screen. A kindred spirit, who was always so close to me. This memory I conveyed to Justine and she enlightened me about twin souls. Beings we choose to come back to this earth with, so we are not alone. Tears welled, I remembered coming through the lights passage with him. My brother, my friend, the other half of my soul.

It was hard to hear, but she explained I was getting stronger, and it was time to let him go. I did not need him anymore. The stronger I got the less room there was within my being to support our connection. I understood. He didn't want to leave. We came to this world together, but only I was manifest in the physical. Justine conveyed that I would need to do a clearing and send him back home to alleviate my symptoms.

He was holding on so tight to my emotional side, in my belly. It was hurting because he was running out of space to live within me. I was becoming my own person, my own energy. I was becoming full and there was no room left for my twin soul. I asked Justine "Could I send him back myself". She said "No, I would need 2 people to assist me, one at my head and one at my feet to keep me grounded throughout the process".

My sister Kathy was someone who I confided in with my many experiences and we shared some together. She would understand. I tried to ring her, but alas to no avail. I left a message to ring me back. I left her no details on what was going on inside of me. A week passed and I started becoming anxious. I knew what I needed to do, but I couldn't get the help I needed. By the time my sister rang me I was beside myself. I blurted out the emergency I was facing. The symptoms were starting to consume me like a flu.

My sister said she was prompted by a close friend of hers to contact me. My sister's friend Veronica asked how I was going. My sister answered "I don't know". Veronica told her that she needed to contact me as something was wrong. Now my sister knew why. I conveyed more of the story to my sister. I was watching a Jane Eyre series on television and one part showed a girl awoken from her sleep calling out a name. The name of the boy she admired. This also happened to me. I had been calling out a name in my sleep that past week. My sister asked what the name was I said "Braxton". My heart dropped as my sister told me of Braxton hicks a term used for false contractions when pregnant. The penny dropped and all fell into place. These cramps were so much like I was having a baby. Although I had not conceived a child yet to fully understand the true entirety of this.

My sister was more than happy to help. I wondered who the other person could be. Who do you ask to assist in such a peculiar dilemma? It definitely needs to be someone open minded and spiritually inclined. My sister raised the idea of a friend of hers named Hilda, who I knew and trusted to be open to the unusual in life. The contact was made, accepted, and a date set. I rang Justine to let her know I had two people who would help. I asked for advice on the clearing process involved. She said I would need to connect on my own first, to the energy I was trying to alleviate. She asked "When I connected to it, what did I see". I described an area in my belly looking like black and sludgy tar. She suggested I buy liquorice straps to resemble this image. She said to connect to the energy beforehand and eat the liquorice to resemble this part of me that I wanted letting go. She said "Do this just before the clearing and let what happens just happen, let it out, be it chanting, running about, whatever happens just let it happen".

The day arrived. My sister and Hilda arrived. I explained to them how I needed to connect to the energy first before I would be ready to release it. I set up my massage table outside in the backyard. My sister decided to be at my feet and Hilda at my head. I told them I would connect to the energy on my own and come back when I felt the time was right.

I got the liquorice straps and put my hand on my belly. I closed my eyes to connect. I felt a rush of energy. My stomach expanded and I stared to eat the liquorice. Many tongues came out of me as I sat on the front porch. I spoke in ways I never knew. Languages and noises that took me over. I had to move. I darted to and fro, metre to metre. I worked the energy up and up until I felt I would explode. It was time.

I went out the back feeling exhausted. In the twenty minutes or so I had been connecting to the energy. I told the girls how tired I felt. They said it showed on my face. I lay down on the massage table. Energy was pulsing up and down through every vein and cell of my body. My sister and Hilda laid their hands on me. My energy became more balanced between them. My body felt like it was floating. My mind connected to a vision. A man hovered down from above and reached out his hand. A young boy came out of my belly and gravitated his hand towards the man's outstretched hand from above. As soon as the hands touched he was gone. Tears filled my eyes. I felt a great loss inside. "I will miss you", I said to him. I came to and both my sister and Hilda had looks of astonishment. Both of them felt different sensations through the process. I felt a lot better, but sad. It was like a piece of me was missing, but I knew it was for the best. I couldn't keep him with me anymore. My sister also witnessed the man that came to retrieve the boy. I let them speak first to relay what they felt from the experience. My *sister's friend Hilda said she was concentrating so hard to keep me grounded here and within myself. She felt the struggle within the release. My sister witnessed the man's appearance as he came to take my twin soul home. She felt the sadness from me as he left.*

The connection with my twin soul was so great, I had to make sure I did not re-open the connection and let him back in. It has taken many years of mind talk and separation to now be able to utter his name once again.

Chapter 11

I set about my next goal, which was to assist young people. I felt that there was a great chance to help make a difference in their lives. I gained my certificate three in community services while studying and working as a carer. I went on to study certificate four in juvenile justice and protective care. My job outline was to assist young people with social, emotional, and behavioural problems, resulting from a break down in their family unit. Children in this situation may exhibit varying degrees of social, emotional, or behavioural difficulty resulting from abuse, neglect, or simply their own unmanageable behaviours. This led them to be taken away from their family unit and put into foster care.

I was now a student with no income. I lived sparingly on a government study grant. This was just enough to pay my tuition fees. I had a little saved, but this was not going to last long. The house I had lived in for the past few years had been sold. I was in desperate need of a place to live, as well as a job. I loved taking drives to the hills. There was a bushwalk with a lovely waterfall. I decided to take myself and Rusty my dog for a day in the country. We had a lovely time, wadding in the fresh water. I then made my way home. I only got as few minutes down the road, when my car started playing up. I lived another forty minutes' drive away. The engine was chugging and coughing, until it came to a complete halt. It stopped just outside the local hotel. I went in to ask to use the phone. I noticed on my way in a sign that said "Bar staff wanted". I am looking for a job. Is this a sign? Well it was a sign, but is this why my car had broken down, here of all places. I arranged a tow truck for the car and then proceeded to ask about the job. It was mainly weekend work, with one night shift per week. This would fit in great, as my week-days were filled up with my youth work *course. I talked myself up to the manager, telling her of my work history. I had waitressing experience and my certificates gained in counselling and community care. The manager laughed and said "Well the counselling one would come in handy, because so many of our patrons want someone to listen to their problems". The manager decided to hire me on the spot. I was asked to start that coming weekend for a week's trial. I agreed. Now all I had to do was find a home. I picked up the local newspaper to look for places to live, while I waited for the tow truck.*

I was a bit perturbed about sharing with strangers. I did find an advertisement from a sixty year old lady who was looking for a border. This sounded like a safe bet. The tow truck arrived and the driver was kind enough to take Rusty and I home on the way to the mechanic. I rang the sixty year old lady who was looking for a border, on arrival home. It was Sunday afternoon. I wanted to find a place to live, near my new job, by that coming Friday. My concern was Rusty as the advertisement said nothing about pets being allowed. The elderly lady was named Joy. She was pleasant to talk to. She was a single lady living with her three year old poodle dog. I told her about my youth work studies on weekdays and the local bar job I had on weekends. I told her that she wouldn't see me much because of this. I then told her that I had a well behaved cattle dog, who I hoped would also be allowed to stay. Joy said she loved dogs and had one of her own. Joy said as long as her dog and mine get along with each other there shouldn't be a problem. Joy agreed to have me move in with Rusty on a trial basis. We would then take it from there. Everything was falling into place. I moved my belongings in on the Friday. I had a good sized room at the back corner of the house, with a view of the yard. The house was fully-fenced so I did not need to worry about Rusty escaping when I was out. The little Poodle dog was so sweet, but quite timid and coy. Rusty was gentle in the greeting process. This helped them to become friends in no time. My first shift at the bar was on Saturday evening, until close. The hotel was only a few blocks away from where I was staying, which made it handy. The hardest thing about a new job is getting used to the routines and how things are done. When working with the public you also have to consider their needs and attitudes too. A bar environment can be welcoming or unforgiving depending on the attitude you present the ever enquiring and at times offensive public. Coming on too stern or strong can gain you instant enemies, while being too meek or forgiving can make you seem a push over. There is a balance that needs to be favoured, which is determined by the patron's influences at the time. I felt this job would be good training in how to deal with peoples behaviours. This could only benefit my management skills when presented with behavioural problems in future youth work.

My first shift at the bar went well. I fitted in nicely. I finished work around 1am that night. I was looking forward to a sleep in. I was woken at 9am by Joy opening the bedroom door wide open. I was perplexed and shocked as to why. I asked Joy if everything was ok. She replied "Yes I was just airing the room". This annoyed me at first. I replied "I didn't finish work until 1am this morning". I thought this would imply to her that I needed to be undisturbed. Joy just went on to say how nice the day was outside. I got up figuring I was not going to get any more sleep. I went to put the jug on to boil for a cup of tea. Joy quickly jumped at me saying "No I am waiting for the water to cool so I can put it into the fridge". Joy then said "I don't drink tap water without boiling it first". "Ok", I said. I decided to get a pot of water to boil for my tea. I went out back to see my dog Rusty, and sat outside to enjoy my cup of tea. I went back inside to ask Joy if she was needing the bathroom. I wanted to have a shower. She said "That's fine but I need to show you what I do with the water". There was a big bucket under the shower which she expected me to stand in to catch the running water. "Oh", was my response. I asked her "Are we on tank water". "No, but I don't like wasting water", she replied. I thought this is a bit much, fair enough if she wants to live this way but I should be allowed to have choice. I had my shower, without the bucket. I decided to take Rusty for a long walk just ten minutes up the road. To the same beautiful waterfall that originally brought us here. I needed to de-stress and cool off.

The longer I stayed with Joy the more eccentric she became. She even tried to get me to join her religious faith. The only time she left the house was to attend these religious meetings. I was happy to have the house to myself for a change. Joy was nice enough, but her quirks started to drive me crazy. I decided that I needed to find another place to live. I asked around work and found two older men who had a spare room. I asked my boss about their characters and reputation. I didn't agree to this prospect until I was sure that there would be no hidden agendas. The living arrangements were great. Both men were out at work when I was home and vice versa. Their *house was on the other side of town, but still only a short distance to work. I became one of the boys, especially when the rugby was on. This is where I learned all about the game. It was fun to watch, especially the reactions of the men when their favourite teams were playing.*

Part of my job at the bar was to listen to people's problems. One afternoon I noticed a man about the same age as me, sitting at the bar. He looked like he was not having a good day. I made small talk. I asked him how his day was. The man told me that he had not been to bed yet. I replied "Gee you did have a good night out". He looked blankly and said "No I just don't want to go home, the woman I live with is doing my head in". I asked why?, The man said "The woman he shares with will make him wait until the water is cooled down in the kettle before he can use it". He went on to say "She doesn't let you sleep, because she opens your bedroom door when she gets out of bed in the morning". I started putting two and two together. I thought, gee this sounds so much like Joy. I asked the man her name, he replied "Joy". I told him that I used to board with her a short while back. I asked if he was staying in the corner bedroom overlooking the back yard. The man said "Yes". This man was living in my old room, putting up with all the problems that I had just left behind. I was totally blown away at the coincidence. I told him that I understood how he was feeling. I suggested that he moved out. I introduced myself to Macca and said if you need someone to talk to you know where I am. Macca thanked me and left soon after this. It was a quiet night, so we shut the bar around 9pm that evening. The manager asked if the staff wanted to come back to her house for a couple of drinks. I was still new to the job and thought it would be a good way to get to know everyone. I was at the manager's house no longer than twenty minutes when I received a call from Macca. I was shocked. I asked how he got my number. He said that he found my number in Joy's phone book. I asked if he was stalking me. Macca said "No I didn't know who else to contact". I asked what was wrong. Macca told me that Joy was walking the street in nothing but her nightie. Macca thought she had lost her mind. I told him to ring the police. Macca said "I don't want to do that as it could set her right off". He was worried about her kicking him out. I told Macca that Joy had a son living in the next town. I encouraged him to ring him to deal with it. Macca said "I can't find the number, I just want to get out of here". I understood Macca's dilemma as Joy could be very intrusive and dominant at times. I asked Macca if he had anywhere to go. Macca said "I don't know many people. He had moved from interstate only a few months earlier. I said "Well I don't normally do this, but I will come and pick you up, you can stay with me for the night". Macca said "Really, would you do that". I replied "Yes I understand what you are going through and I could have done with some help when the same thing was happening to me". I let Macca know I was sharing a house with two other men, so no funny business. Macca assured me that he was not after anything like that from me. I said "Ok then, do you have a car? Macca said that he didn't. I said "I could come and pick you up, but I am not coming to Joy's house". Macca said "I will meet you in the car park where you work". I left the manager's home and thanked her for inviting me. The manager asked if I was ok. I said "Yes, just a mini-crisis that I have offered to help with". I laughed. I picked up Macca from the car park. I heard all about Joy's antics. Apparently she said that Macca was crazy, I laughed and said "Gee that's calling the kettle black". I told Macca he could stay just one night as it was not my house. We stayed up talking until the other two men came home. I made Macca a bed up on the couch and wished him well in finding a new place to live. We had so much in common. He seemed like a really nice guy, who was stuck in the wrong place, at the wrong time. I woke to find Macca had gone. I felt good about helping another with the same distress that I had gone through. That afternoon there was a knock at the door It was Macca with a ruck sack and a worried look on his face. I asked if he was ok. Macca said that Joy had thrown all his belongings onto the street. I thought how out of character that was for her. I knew she was a bit kooky, but I didn't think she would be that unkind. Macca asked "Can I stay just a few days' tops, until I found a place to live". I told him that it is not my house and that the other men would not be keen. Macca asked "Can I stay in your room, on the floor, they wouldn't need to know". I replied "If they found out you stayed they would flip their lids and probably kick me out". Macca said "I promise I will be good, no funny business and I will be as quiet as a mouse". I sighed and said "Ok, but you had better find another place to live quick smart, my necks on the line here". It was nearing 5pm and the start of my shift at the bar. I knew the other two men would be home soon. I told Macca not to touch anything and to be quiet. I said "The two men that live here will eat you for breakfast. Macca said "I will probably just sleep, as it had been a turbulent few days". I arrived back from work that night to find Macca asleep in my bed. I was not impressed. I asked "What are you doing in my bed". Macca said "He only laid down for a minute and fell asleep". I said "Well where am I meant to sleep". Macca said "I promise I will keep to my side of the bed". Macca hadn't shown any signs of being untrustworthy so far, so I took his word for it. I got into bed. I was almost asleep when Macca asked "Can we cuddle. I replied "Yeah right just cuddle". He said "No I mean it, I just want to be close to you". I said "Well you're in my bed how close do you want to be". He laughed and said "You're funny". He asked me to lay in his arms. I did, and fell off to sleep. I woke in the morning thinking how nice it was to be comforted. Macca woke up and said "He would go and visit a guy he had met, to see if he knows of anywhere he can stay". I said "That would be great as I feel like I am harbouring a fugitive". We laughed. I got a phone call from Macca the day after, to say he had found a place to live. I enquired as to where. Macca told me it was with the guy he spoke of, renting a room with him the guy's girlfriend. Macca gave me the address and asked me to visit sometime. It was about a week later. I decided to visit Macca in his new place. It was a twenty five minute drive away. I arrived and was surprised to see a black wooden cat figure on the wall. It was exactly the same as what my mum used to make and have in her house. With this familiarity I felt at home. I took this as being a sign that all would be well. Macca's mate and his girlfriend were lovely, they made me feel very much at home. I had been working at the bar almost a year now. I was close to finishing my course to become a youth worker. Macca and I had developed a close bond over a short time. I often wondered if Macca boarding with Joy was just a coincidence, or fate. We clicked. It was like he could read how I felt, and what I needed. I appreciated having someone that understood me. Macca asked if I wanted to come live with him. I was overwhelmed with the fact he felt so close to me, after such a short time. I told him I would like to finish my course first, so that I don't have to work at the bar anymore. We agreed that I would move in three weeks' time, when my course had finished. I had been working so hard the last year clearing my grief, staying positive, and asserting myself to a new start. It felt good to also be falling in love. The day arrived for me to move in. I finished my job at the bar, to then take on the role as a youth worker. I had a new career, a home, and a boyfriend. My life seemed dandy, and I was so happy with my personal achievements. I moved my belongings into Macca's room and sat down on the bed for a breather. I closed my eyes for a second and saw a coloured geometric symbol. Macca asked "What was that". I smiled and said "What". He said "You saw something". I laughed. I replied "Yeah sometimes I see symbols". Macca looked so serious and questioned me on what it looked like. I said "They are hard to remember, it happens so quickly". Then it dawned on me. I asked him "How did you know what I saw, can you read my mind"? Macca replied "I can pick up on people's energy". I was excited. "Me too", I said. "Wow another one like me", I said out aloud and laughed. Macca intrigued me. I had never met anyone like me before. That night on retiring to bed, Macca seemed distant. He did not want to fall asleep with me. Ok I thought, we live together now, of course things are going to be different. That night I had quite a disturbing dream.

I found myself outside a house. I could feel Macca was inside, so I went in the front door. I was then surrounded by a group of men and woman in their early twenties. Macca was one of them. I tried to talk to the group. I said "Macca does not need to be here and neither do all of you". It was like they were in transit, a holding station of energies. The more I tried to converse and open them up to the possibility of letting Macca go, they became more hostile. I started to feel unsafe. I decided to leave and walk out the front door. The group followed me outside and surrounded me once more. They were all vying around me. I heard them talking in tongues. They were trying hard to invade my psyche. I ran as fast as I could, away from them. I was drawn to an automated money machine, to then see Macca's face protruding out of the screen saying "Give me money, give me money". This scared me even more. I ran as fast as I could. I brushed past a big cycad plant. One of the fronds slit the side of my neck. It started to bleed. I held my hand over the area to try and stop the bleeding. I woke from the dream in the early hours of the morning. I saw Macca beside me, resting on his arm watching me sleep. Macca asked "How is your neck"? with a wry grin. My chest dropped to my stomach. How did he know what my dream was about? I automatically knew he was a part of this. Macca had gotten into my dreams. I was petrified that someone had the power to do this. I pretended I didn't know what he was talking about. He then asked what I had dreamt about. I said "I can't remember". My mind was racing, *not knowing how I was going to get out of this situation. I decided that I was not safe around him and set about distancing myself. I had a shower and readied myself for the day. I made up the excuse that I needed to work that day. This was when I set about finding another place to live. I found a share house on the coast, with a school teacher and truck driver. They were standard people, no alarm bells rang. The school teacher Joline had a dog, so it was fine for me to have my dog Rusty. We all agreed that I could move in on the weekend. It was Thursday so that left only one more night with Macca. My heaviness lightened as I had found another place to live. Now all I had to do was convince Macca to leave me alone. I returned back to the house to find Macca all chirpy and wanting to go out. I was hesitant. I knew that I didn't want to go, but I was also scared to say no. Macca wanted to take a drive down the coast to watch the sunset. This sounded nice in theory. I thought this might be a good chance to talk to him about leaving. Macca drove the car. I had an uneasy vibe, like he was going to suddenly crash on purpose. When we passed a large set of gum trees I could feel a magnetic pull. It was as if I could feel the thought dart across his mind. I looked at him. I saw a sinister grin. His eyes were dark and his face was slightly screwed up. I delved inside of myself for positive conversation to throw off his train of thought. Anything that would change his view. I managed to spark his memory about a funny time which made him laugh. Relief surged through my being like a deep breathe. Macca decided to stop at a bottle store to get a couple of drinks. I figured this was my chance to get out of the car and talk him into letting me drive. I was not going to get back in otherwise. I made up a story of a really nice place I knew of along the coast. I told him I would need to drive for it to be a surprise. Macca agreed. Macca was stared at me as I got into the driver's seat. I smiled at him and said "Are you ready"? I said this with as much positive enthusiasm as I could muster. I went to drive off and got confused. I wasn't sure which way I was supposed to go. Macca was laughing. He asked "What was wrong with you". I said "I don't know I can't think straight". Macca stopped laughing and became serious. He pointed in the direction of the coast. He said "That is enough games or we will never get there". It felt like I was washed over, blurred, hazy, and disorientated, until he withdrew his gaze. I didn't like what was happening to me, nor the control he seemed to have over me when he chose to. I figured my best defence would be to stay neutral, and act as though I* was unaware of what he was doing. I was so uncomfortable having to play this game to be safe, but I had no other choice. We made it to the coast. I thought of my sister as she lived near-by. I had no right to bring this fright into my sister's world. I had to sort this out for myself. Macca and I parked with a view of the ocean. I spoke to Macca about my new job as a mentor for troubled youth. I mentioned how difficult it can be to find solutions for them if I am not clear within myself. I said "My new boss has stated that employees need to lead uncomplicated lives because the youth we deal with have a lot of problems. I didn't dare tell him I was moving until we were home safely. I was using every form of factual evidence to back up my story to leave. I knew I had to keep the conversation going to keep Macca's mind from wandering to that dark place within him. I managed to do this all the way back, until we were safely indoors once again. The other couple were also home that evening, so I felt comfort in the extra company. I told Macca that I didn't want to have a boyfriend because my new job was going to take up most of my time and energy. I stated that I needed to stay focussed if I was going to help make a difference for these kids. Macca started to put me down, verbally, telling me I was not good enough for this job. I said "I have worked hard to get this job and I am not going to lose it now by making bad decisions". Macca started yelling. This alerted the other couple to come to my aide. They were not happy with Macca's verbal abuse or his unsafe manner toward me. They asked him to leave. I told the couple I had found another place to live. I thanked them for their hospitality. They apologised for Macca's behaviour. I replied "You are not responsible for his actions, he is". I packed up my things for the next day's move. I then tried to sleep. I was too anxious to sleep. Morning came and I set off to my new home, leaving the past behind.

Out of innocence, naivety and wanting to help another in the most peculiar of coincidences, I learnt how vulnerable I was. This lesson taught me about the varying planes of existence. Depending on what we emanate mentally and emotionally. This can characterize what is drawn to us. Be it positive or negative. There is a scale of balance, tipping in favour of how we think and see ourselves. Depression, substance abuse, low self-esteem, or any other form of spirit dampening, can lead us on a path of self-destruction. It is when within this sphere we are open to negative influence. By trolling the depths of misery we are walking the dark road.

This is where you may find those beings that are no longer physical. They exist within a certain vibrational frequency. If we radiate anything close to that frequency, they can pick up on it, like a beacon. It is at this point that the beings from the lower realms can infiltrate our awareness. They are beings that have lost all hope. It is for this reason they latch onto those in disparity. It strengthens what they already feel. They use the suffering of others to empower themselves. Using influencing thoughts and actions, they feed your damp state with even more heaviness. This in effect can drive us to the edge of our own existence. It is at this moment, like a clap of thunder, we realize hopefully how lost we are. This shock is usually enough to prompt us to talk to someone or get help.

Emotionally, I had been doing the work to heal, yet there was still an empty place within. It was this hollow that allowed me to be fooled by Macca. The want of someone to see me, feel me, know me, like my mother did. This was no coincidence, but a teaching on loving thy self. I needed to identify with this wound. This enabled me to heal and close the opening which allowed me to become so emotionally flippant with my feelings. I was making my way, but I was still climbing.

This prompted me to join MMA mixed martial arts. I then went on to learn the Yang Mian System of Kung-Fu. I still practise to this day. It has become a part of my life. I am now in control of my nervous system through the connection to my dan-tien, energy centre. This has produced emotional balance and internal power. I spent my spare time keeping fit, nurturing myself and keeping out of harm's way.

Chapter 12

I started my youth work with a renewed vigour. I was determined to be a pivotal influence in the lives of the young people that were assigned to me. I came to realize through working with these young people, that shattered emotions could led to shattered realities.

I had night shift with a sweet young girl who I escorted to counselling sessions on a weekly basis. When I saw her that afternoon she warned me that she was not the same at night time. I didn't understand what she meant. She went from sweet to savage in one evening. She was so frightened of falling asleep. I saw her pain. The little miss tried everything in the book to upset me. Throwing food at me, along with her fists and verbal abuse. Devilish in the drive of pushing me away. Too scared to let anyone close. This state endured until the wee hours of the morning, until the little darling ran out of fuel. She finally put herself into bed. I went in to check on her. She looked up at me and said "You probably won't even say goodnight now". I pulled up the covers and kissed her on the forehead. "Sweet dreams", I said. I was exhausted. I kept myself balanced, open and caring throughout the ordeal. I laid on the couch and closed my eyes. I felt the sensation of a giant hand gently rest its palm on my head. I was then cleared of all the stress of that night. Every ounce of stress disappeared. I became so clear, calm and at peace. I thanked the being that healed me and fell into a peaceful sleep. This experience has never left me, I felt touched by an Angel.

I helped and supported many children in my role as youth worker. Just like all of us young people need us to listen and care. Bad behaviour is not instinctual, it develops. My job was to give them allowance to be. To let out what ailed them, in the hope they would find strength to confront the cause.

I worked with youth for almost three years. It became harder to let go the longer I stayed. I became emotionally attached to a couple of them. They still to this day have a place in my heart and mind. I became disgruntled with the system in relation to the young people we were trying to help.

I felt like my hands were tied. I got to a stage where I could give no more, considering the boundaries these young people found themselves in. A wise male mentor of mine explained that nothing can take away the pictures these young people have in their mind. It is like a soldier who has come back from war. No one would understand what he has seen or experienced. It is the same for the young people. It is not something you want to talk about. When rehashed or unearthed in various therapies, all it does is bring up the same feelings. To let go takes understanding. To understand takes time and experience. To forgive. That is what frees us from the situation. One of the hardest things to do, especially if an authority figure such as a parent or guardian is to blame. In situations like this, it is not the youth that need the help, but the adults. We need to help the adults become better role models and assist them to open doors of opportunity to advance their self-worth.

I gave my resignation as a youth worker and set about looking for other job roles involving helping and caring. I trolled the local newspapers. I came across a job doing private care for a forty year old man with autism. I had never worked in the disability sector. I felt it was time for a change. I contacted the parents of the man. They asked how much I knew about negative behaviours. I alerted them to the fact my last job was working with young people who had behavioural problems. They asked if I would like to come to the house for an interview and meet David, the man who I would be caring for. I agreed.

I arrived at the house to be greeted by the parents. I heard moaning from down the hall. Greg the father of David laughed and said "It sounds like David wants to meet you". I was apprehensive. Greg outlined David's needs before I got to meet him. David had challenging behaviours of self-harm. He wore arm splints to prevent him from hitting himself in the head. He was likened to a toddler by his father as he could not feed or toilet himself. He wore nappies and needed to be hand fed. David could walk but only short distances, so a wheelchair was used on outings. David was non-verbal but very expressive with vocal tones and physical indicators. He would rock back and forth if not in a good mood. He loves nursery rhymes.

He had many musical toys. This kept him content when playing. He was very quick to move and able to swipe or pick things up as soon as he saw them. Greg explained that David only responds to one word at a time and that he does not understand sentences. I took all this in. Greg asked "Do you still want the job"? I accepted. "I do like a challenge", I said with a smile. Greg went to get David. When I saw David I couldn't believe how big he was. He was thickly built and stood a good three inches taller than myself. David was coy and didn't want to make eye contact with me. I spoke to him like I would any other person I had met for the first time. I told him that we would become good friends and that I was coming to his house to look after him. David started whacking himself violently in the head with his fists. David had a big lump on his head from beating himself. Susan, David's mother explained that they let him have time out in his room and take his splints off if he is even tempered. Greg told me that meeting new people caused anxiety for David. Greg said he would need to put David's arm splints back on. Greg asked if I would like to see how that's done. I said "Yes". I followed behind while Greg ushered David to his bedroom. David had a piece of trellis drilled onto one wall in his bedroom. The wall had all his musical toys tied to the wooden slats with ribbon. Greg explained that if they are not tied down David will throw them around. Greg lay David on his single bed. David was moaning and throwing himself all over the place, trying to get up. Greg yelled "No, stop that". This subdued David slightly, but he still was struggling. Greg explained that I may need to use my body weight to hold him down while I put the splints on. Greg showed me by straddling his body across David leaving one arm free to put the splint on. The splint looked like a cast, with Velcro straps. It went from his wrist to just under the armpit. This stopped David from bending his elbow and belting himself in the head. It was quite an arduous task watching Greg put on the splints. Greg said "Don't be afraid to use force to restrain David, he has to know who is boss, otherwise he won't listen to you". Greg explained that David's splints will need adjusting throughout the day, as they slide down if the Velcro is not tight. David calmed down after his splints were on. It was as if he was relieved that he couldn't hurt himself anymore. David got up from his bed and sat on the floor in front of the trellis where his toys were hanging. He grabbed his drinking bottle which was tied with a long ribbon and took a sip, he then threw it when he had finished. Greg laughed and said "That is why we tie his things down. Greg told me David always had a bottle of drink available to him. Greg said if I take him out to just tie it to his wheelchair. David's mother warned me not to wear dangly earrings or necklaces while working with David as he had a habit of grabbing them and not letting go. There was so much to get used to, but first of all I had to get used to David. I kept David's environment familiar for the first couple of weeks, by staying at his home. This gave me a chance to understand David's routines, behaviours and attitudes. David was attached to his bottle, always drinking it throughout the day. He was a fussy eater and I found his tongue muscle was so strong. At times he was able to prevent food from passing into his gullet. He would go through stages of not allowing himself to eat. You just had to wait until his mood changed. I found that singing to him helped shift his aggravation. When David heard you singing his eyes would soften. He had a smile that would lighten up his face. David flung his arms around often, which loosened the Velcro on his arm splints. I felt hostile having to hold him down to readjust them. It was like he was possessed. David was so restricted, almost trapped in this malfunctioning physical form. I got to witness the battle and the beauty within each day of his care. I progressively became more confident in reading his cues in relation to his needs. The next step was to take him out of the house. We started by taking walks around his neighbourhood. David really enjoyed free time in nature. He could be quite swift in his moving about, but would also just plonk himself down on the ground when he did not want to move. Some of the places he sat were at time inappropriate, especially when he sat on a bull-ants nest. My quick thinking strength came out of nowhere that day to move him. My work was to make this little soul happy. In the early months of his care, I had no reason to be concerned with my safety. One particular day when we parked at the beach, that all changed. David was in the backseat of the car, this was a must considering he wanted to touch everything. David placed his hand on my head. I thought, oh nice he is giving me a pat. David then slid his hand down my neck and grabbed at the hoop necklace I was wearing. He tugged it back towards himself. I became scared. I yelled sternly "Let go". "His eyes looked into mine blankly". Then it hit me. I had seen those same eyes, in my dream the night before. The feeling, the dream, the story, all came flooding back. I dreamt I was working as a nurse in a morgue. I was asked to deliver a body, with an identity card to the administrations nurse. The body was on a wheeled stretcher fully covered in a white sheet. I took note of the identification card which read, "Deceased male, motorbike accident". I rounded the corner and caught site of the administration nurse. The sheet had become caught in one of the wheels. It had been pulled away from the dead man's face. I went about untangling the sheet from the wheel. The dead man's eyes opened, stared into mine and then he sat up. I lost it with fear and terror. I throw the identification card toward the administration nurse. The nurse asked "Who I was admitting today". I replied "I don't know he is supposed to be dead". I then ran away. I woke up not remembering a thing, until I saw those same eyes looking at me. It was David. David still had hold of my necklace. I said to him "I know who you are, David let go". He stared into my eyes, then laughed. I said "You don't scare me and don't ever touch me like that again". David sat motionless and looked out the window. The day was nearing an end so I dropped David back home. The dream kept playing over in my mind. I wondered whether people born with severely debilitating disabilities are paying off their life karma. Limited expression does not mean limited cognition. I truly believe that could be why David tried to self-harm and forbid himself from eating. Can you imagine coming back into a body with limited communication skills, but knowing and feeling so much, yet restricted in what can be shared. David battled with himself each day to exist.

I loved working with David over the next few years. It was at the end of this time I realized how tiring this caring position was. Every moment you had to have your wits about you. He could not be left alone for longer than a few minutes, even if I needed to go to the toilet. If you were not fast enough, he would have made a right old mess of something he got his hands on. I came to a point where I felt I could do no more for David. When you lose inspiration for your work that is the time to leave.

Chapter 13

I started looking for a new job. I found a job advertised in the local paper to work for a man with Autism. I had experienced autistic tendencies while working with David. Change can be hard for them to deal with. Anything new has to be introduced slowly and regularly for a familiar comfort to occur. Steps needed to be set up both visually and verbally. I gained entry to the job via an introductory course on Autism. I learnt key aspects on how someone with Autism calculates new information. Charts were advised to show daily tasks to the person we would be working with. This prepared them for what was next, so there would be no upsetting surprises. They needed plenty of time to get used to any new venture. It was not the fact they had trouble grasping new ideas, it was the fact that they already had so much going on within themselves. The example of a supermarket was used. When someone with Autism enters a supermarket or any public place their senses are flooded with stimuli. Their senses are so heightened that they can hear the lady at the checkout rattling through the change in her purse to pay. The harsh iridescent lights illuminate all the products on the shelves. The sound of the grocery scanners, people on cell phones, and ladies with strong perfume, are all stoppers of focus to the task at hand. It would be overwhelming to distinguish between all this information and attend to the task at hand.

I secured a job with a man named Ross. He lived in a residential home by himself with 24 hour care. There had to be two carers working with him at all times. This was due to his physically violent outbreaks. I was under the impression he would be similar to David, with his self-harm outbreaks. I arrived at Ross's house for my first buddy shift. I knocked on the door. I could hear Ross all heightened, laughing loudly, with long high pitched vocal noises. One of the female carers greeted me, while the other woman had Ross arm in arm. I was ushered quickly past Ross and into a secure area. The kitchen was enclosed with a wire screen, like a cyclone fence, reinforced with a metal bar frame. The locking door was made of the same materials. Once I was inside the other carer let go of Ross's arm and quickly made her way in, through the door. I was told to never leave any doors unlocked, it was for mine and Ross's own safety. I watched Ross as he started talking to himself. He was quite tall and thinly built. To look at him you would not think he was in need of high care. He could walk, talk, shower, feed and toilet himself, like everyone else. I asked the two woman carer's how long they had been working with Ross. Their reply was too long. They said "It may sound harsh, but don't let your guard down for a minute as he can be violent". One woman told me how she was attacked when getting out of the toilet. She felt that Ross stalked her. They described Ross as calculating. They said "He will watch your routines, gain your trust and then wham, he will get you". I was a bit put off by their comments. I thought they probably have been in the job too long. I heard what they were saying, but I also felt I could help Ross. Ross could hear all the negative comments being said about him. I didn't think that was fair or kind. I mentally projected to Ross the words "Its ok I don't think like them". Within moments Ross verbally relayed back the exact same words I had said mentally to him. He then went off into his own world by talking to himself. I was excited. He had heard me. We had a connection. I was shown Ross's routines for the day. He went out for a walk in the morning, if his mood was stable. This was after his breakfast and his medication was taken. He was medicated three times a day. This did little to dull his enthusiastic drive to dart, move and talk to himself. He seldom engaged with us, unless he wanted something such as food, or a favourite toy, or game. He showered at night and was helped to bed like a sweet young boy. Another new lady named Marg started with me. We were both new to the job with Ross. We had heard all the horror stories about Ross from previous staff. We were yet to see such a display. It was on the third day when Marg and I were out walking with Ross that we noticed the change. Marg and I were either side of Ross, arm in arm. Ross spotted a man and his dog coming toward us. He started to wriggle and try to get away. He was making high pitched noises at regular intervals. He was eyeballing the man coming toward us. We both forcefully had to hold him.

We were advised to take him home if this happened, as he was a threat to the public. I told Ross we would take him home if he kept up this behaviour. Ross calmed physically, but the sounds were still there. It was not safe to take him out like that. We were told he had attacked a passer by one morning, by lunging at him and scratching his face. We were asked to take Ross out on drives if we felt he could be trusted, and if we felt safe. A week had passed and Ross hadn't caused us too much trouble. We decided to take him out in the work van. There always had to be a carer in the back with him in case his behaviour escalated. It was advised to take snacks with us. This was so Ross could be distracted if he seemed like he was going to act up. Ross enjoyed all the scenery as we drove along. This amused him on the twenty minute drive to visit wild kangaroo's. When we stopped the van Ross quickly got up and tried to push past me to open the door. I said "No Ross, we have to wait for Marg". Marg opened the sliding door of the van once Ross took a step back. I held one of Ross's arms and Marg held the other. There was no one around except grazing Kangaroo's. Ross said he needed to go to the toilet. We walked over to the ablution block and escorted him in. Ross shrugged at our arms as he opened the toilet door. Fair enough I thought, some privacy. Marg and I waited outside the door. Ross was taking ages. We tried to verbally engage with him, but with no response. Just as we were wondering how to get him out, Ross flung open the door and ran. Marg and I chased after him. A young family were parked close to the ablution block. Luckily they saw the commotion and stayed in their car until we caught up to Ross. Ross was laughing hysterically with blank eyes and a dark stare. "That's it you're going home Ross, you have blown it", I said. His laughing stopped and he just stared at me. I said "Ross is a good man, he listens to Marg and me". I tried my best to instil a positive demeanour in Ross before we got back into the van. In these sorts of situations you have to make sure that the person has de-escalated their behaviour, otherwise they are not safe to themselves or you. Marg got some snacks from her bag for Ross. We walked ever so slowly and gently back to the van. I got into the back of the van with Ross again. Marg did ask if I wanted to drive, but I felt more confident that I could read Ross's cues. It was the longest twenty minutes of my life. Every time Ross looked like he was losing interest in the drive and focused on me, I would give him a snack. It was like he was calculating his next move, you could see it in his eyes. Before he got too far along, I would shift his focus with the snack. This was starting to wear thin after the tenth or eleventh time. I knew I had to remain calm, otherwise my mood would encourage Ross to act up. I made up a song about how handsome and nice he was. This gave the trip a false sense of goodness. I hoped the song would sink into Ross's mind, rather than the negative influence which could take him over without warning. We arrived back at the house, all in one piece. Ross was happy to be back and excited about checking the mail box. Ross and I got the mail, while Marg unlocked the door. Ross was a different person. He focussed on the task at hand and repeated what I said. I had a running commentary on the way to the letterbox and back to the door. Every door had to be locked behind Ross. I felt sorry for him and wondered if he was getting enough stimulation. I thought, perhaps he is bored that is why he acts up and lashes out. I just had to do my job as I was told. Marg and I chatted that night after we put Ross to bed. We expressed to each other how sweet Ross was. We questioned his past and wondered whether that had anything to do with his behaviour. We were going to find out as Ross's family were visiting the next day for his birthday. The family arrived and the smile on Ross's face was priceless. He was so excited to see them. I felt bad having to lock the doors behind them. Ross's father asked if Ross could come out the back with them. Ross's father said "I will be responsible for him, we just want to spend some private time with him". Marg and I agreed. Ross's mum, dad, and brother sat with him on the back patio. Marg and I were out of sight, but within ear range in case we were needed. Ross was talking candidly about happy family memories. He was engaged in the conversation, replying, and interjecting at the appropriate times. It was a new Ross. One I did not know existed. When Ross was in care he would talk and answer himself, like there was someone else in the room. He had names for each person he would talk to. I even asked Ross who a couple of them were as the names became familiar to me. Ross would speak for them and then he would reply to himself. They seemed to have different characters. Ross would change according to with whom he was speaking. It seemed a struggle for Ross sometimes not to listen to what they were saying. Ross would get angry and yell "NO, I CAN'T, I WONT". After two weeks I noticed a pattern forming between the characters he would talk to, their names, and his behaviour. Ross's family left and were happy with their time with Ross. You could see in Ross's face how he loved to engage with his family. After they *left Ross went back into talking mode. He sat with the present his parents gave him. It was a plastic twelve pin bowling set. Ross's father assured me that Ross would be fine to play with it. It wasn't Ross I was worried about, it was us. Ross was sitting rocking to and fro, when his voice started to rise. He was looking at the kitchen barrier and then the plastic pins. Ross then yelled out "TOILET", in a whiney, high pitched voice. We had to leave the safety of the barrier and open the door to take him to the toilet. I discussed with Marg who was going to take him to the toilet. One of us had to stay in case we needed to call our supervisor for assistance. I said I would go. I looked out and Ross was disappeared from our view. The pins were all over the floor. I couldn't be sure if he had one in his hand, ready to clobber me over the head. I was nervous. I called out to Ross and asked "Do you still need to go to the toilet?" I heard nothing. Marg and I queried each other in regards to my safety? I couldn't be sure I would be safe. It felt like Ross was waiting just around the corner to ambush me. I did not feel safe to take him to the toilet. I went behind the closed in kitchen to the joining office at the back. I rang the supervisor. I had just picked up the receiver to dial, when I heard an almighty thud. Marg yelled out "Ross has run at the barrier full pelt and fallen down laughing". I replied "I told you he was not in a good mood". Ross changed his voice to sweet and coy. He then asked for a cookie. He was standing in front of the barrier door, using his hand to pretend to grab for a cookie. He started repeating the word "Cookie", over and over. Each time his voice was becoming more hostile and high pitched. I said to Ross "You just want us to open the door". Ross looked at me and swung a hit at the barrier in front of me. He yelled "COOKIE". He then fell to the floor. He lifted his legs and started to kick the barrier door as hard as he could. He kicked it so hard and so many times, that I was sure he was going to injure himself or eventually break through. I rang our supervisor Tom to inform him what was happening. Tom could hear Ross in the background. Tom asked "Can we get out safely". There was no other door within the enclosure only a window that was in the back office. Tom said "Don't let Ross see or hear you". The supervisor would be over in about 1ten minutes. Those ten minutes became horrendously nerve wracking. Ross kept thrashing at the door with his feet. I said to Marg "If Ross gets in I am not sure what he will do". Marg agreed. There was silence. We waited and listened. Nothing. Marg asked "Should we see if Ross is ok, he may have injured* himself". We quietly peeked around the door frame to see Ross ready and loaded with a hefty bash of his legs to break down the door. Marg and I knew that the door was not going to hold. I panicked. I said "We have got to get out the window, help me". The noise alerted Ross to our presence. Ross yelled out in a sweet, volatile voice "TOILET", then laughed a sinister laugh. I got the fly screen off the office window. Marg opened it by turning the spinning handle at an urgent pace. Ross started banging on the door again with his feet. It was starting to creak and weaken with each bout. I got out first, then I helped Marg. Once outside we started feeling better. We did not feel trapped. I thought this is how Ross must feel. I then flicked my thoughts to the back door. I asked Marg "Is the back door locked"? Marg was not sure. Neither one of us remembered locking it after Ross's family left. I said to Marg "We will have to check". We crept under the window of the lounge room where Ross was. It was so quiet in there. I was really worried he had hurt himself. I whispered to Marg "Check if the door is locked, I will see if Ross is ok". I lifted my head to see Ross standing, looking at the barrier. He spotted me out of the corner of his eye and started to raise his voice into long high pitched groans. Ross turned to see Marg. He then ran for the door. I yelled to Marg "Is the door locked"? Marg said "No I will lock it now". "There's no time he is coming", I said. Ross burst out the back door. Marg and I ran into the garage. Ross picked up a chair and threw it at us. He was backing us into the corner. I turn to see a door that leads outside to the front of the house. Marg and I rush over. We turn the door handle and lock it from the outside. We hear Ross laugh wickedly and thrash on the door. We caught our breath just before being greeted by our supervisor. He asked "Has Ross calmed down"? I reply "Do you think we would both be outside if he had". Tom went to open the garage door. I said "No Ross will be waiting on the other side of the door". I gave Tom my keys and said "Go in the front way". Tom asked "Are you both ok"? I said "No we don't get paid danger money". Tom said "I will debrief with you both after I have calmed Ross down". Marg and I agreed that the amount of stress we incurred, plus the threatening situation, with almost no escape, was not what we signed up for. I said to Marg "There at least needs to be another door so staff can make a fast get away if needed". I heard Tom inside calling out to Ross. Tom made it round to the other side of the garage door. He coaxed Ross back inside. Ross smashed on the garage door one last time and *sniggered away. Tom gave Ross some extra medication to mildly sedate him. Tom asked "Are you both ok to keep working or do you need the night off"? I said "I don't know about you Marg but that was the last straw for me, I will not be returning to this job again". Tom asked "Are you resigning". "Effective now", I said. Tom wanted to know if there was anything he could do to make me reconsider my resignation. I said "No, I cannot work under these nerve wracking and threatening conditions".*

Still to this day I question whether Ross was schizophrenic or autistic.

I took a two week break before looking for a new job. My nervous system was frazzled and I needed time to regain strength. I thought about what I wanted to do next. I enjoyed working with people, but I did not want to be put under so much stress. I wished that I could have the same wages per week, with less manual hours. My dream.

Chapter 14

I *spotted another job advertised in the disability sector. I was a little perturbed about going for the position until I knew exactly what it entailed. I attended the interview. I was relieved to hear that the company was different. They looked at each client as able, and did not limit them to their disability title. The job was to encourage, support and inspire social participation, while teaching life skills. I was to support two woman with Autistic tendencies. The woman lived independently. They rented their own home and attended work Monday to Friday. I was asked to meet them after work Tuesday to Friday. I asked to help them prepare dinner, make their lunch for work the following day, budget their money, and encourage positive relations both socially and publicly. Anything they wanted to do they could, it was just a matter of planting the seed. We then set about mapping and understanding the steps needed to be successful. The women needed routine and inspiration. It is all good to assert yourself to a task, but if you're inspired by the outcome there is more willingness to participate. That was the key. Cooking, cleaning, shopping, going to work, all these tasks can become mundane. But not for someone with Autism. It is the routines that give them comfort and build their confidence. There is a sense of achievement which can be built on. We wrote up a daily roster that we put on the fridge for them both to see each day. The roster outlined the different tasks needed to run the house. The women alternated the tasks each day. The jobs were discussed and agreed upon by both of them. No good making a roster if no one agrees to do the work. The women had complete control over their money. This was fantastic if spending was calculated at regular intervals. I had to intervene initially with a budget. This made the women aware of their spending in relation to paying bills and their weekly* expenses. The company I worked for were all about letting them make their own mistakes. I could only advise and guide them. In the end the decision was theirs. When they didn't have enough money for their food, shopping, or there was a final warning to pay the electricity bill, this prompted their awareness. We do not learn without example. A budget was worked out and the women used internet banking to allocate their money each week into separate automatic payments.

The women were chalk and cheese. They were nothing like each other, yet they had lived together for years. Charlie was quiet and a bit shy. It took me a long time to build a close relationship with her. Regina on the other hand was larger than life and loved being a drama queen. Regina did have her down times, when she would turn inward and shut down. She would come right again after a few days of talking to herself, with limited social interaction. It was only after a bond was formed with these women did I truly start to understand their life view. Charlie was not quiet at all. She was loud, very loud when happy and excited. She was very intuitive and knew how to gage the emotional response of any person she interacted with. This took the guess work out of life. This in turn secured her safe boundaries when in public places. She showed no physical indicators of having a disability and neither did Regina. I think this was the hardest to comprehend for the general public. They could see no reason why either woman could act so differently. Regina had a habit of throwing her arms up and swaying side to side with a groan, in both troubled and happy times. This was her way to release the emotion. Because her senses were already so heightened, it did not take much to tip her over the edge. She was never violent, but she could get verbally abusive. Over time this subsided. I was able to talk her down and find out the trigger situation that caused her melt down. The connection that was built between Regina and I allowed her to open up more. She showed me more of her personality. Sometimes out of the blue she would talk to herself. Her conversations were like she was talking to an unwelcome visitor. This happened at irregular intervals. Each time I saw this occur, Regina would get in a bad mood. I noted this change to myself and just observed the pattern of behaviour. Once I was alerted to this change, I observed more closely when the change occurred. It was then I noticed a dark fog next to her at the onset of this character change. I asked Regina "Is someone bothering you"? She replied "Yes". I told Regina to tell them to go away. Her face started looking cross. I asked Regina "Who is this person that makes you angry"? Regina said "I don't know, they hang around me all the time". I asked Regina if she likes them hanging around her. She said "No". I said "Well you will have to tell them to leave you alone". Regina said "Leave me alone". I noticed the dark mass retreat a short distance. I then concentrated on lifting Regina's energy and made a joke saying "You have plenty of friends, we don't need those ones, go away". "Yeah go away", Regina said. She then started on a different tangent to do with the TV. Success, we had averted a full melt down. My job with Regina became more about lifting her self-esteem and outlook so that there was no room for darkness. It was an ongoing battle, but at least she was aware that she had the power to control how she felt.

I only worked about twenty hours a week with the women after the initial life changes had been set up. I had received my wish, to work less hours, with the same pay. This allowed me time to delve into my spiritual interests.

Chapter 15

I started work on weekends at Spiritual fairs. I did healings and spirit drawings. This is where I met my Maori sis Jennifer. My interest in her was sparked by the tattoo she had on her chin. I got the sense it was family orientated and sure enough it was. It was a legacy passed down from her grandmother. We became friends and I started working with Jennifer at a spiritual shop on Mondays. The shop was owned by a friend of hers.

About a year passed where things were some-what quiet?

I was given a link to an earth chakra site by a friend. It stated different areas across the globe that housed major energy sites. In March the following year, there was an energy shift within these earth chakras. New Zealand's central north island housed one of them. It was my birthday in March, so I decided to treat myself to a New Zealand adventure. I enlisted the advice of my spiritual sis Jennifer. She was originally from the north Island of New Zealand. I asked about the where, what and how's of the place. It was from Jennifer that I first heard the story of the Children of the Mist, or Patupaiarehe, meaning faerie folk. I had decided on a camping holiday. Jennifer warned me, that if I heard little footsteps or giggles at night, to not leave the tent and follow them. She said "They are small mischievous beings that can put you in situations where it is easy to injure yourself". It was folklore passed down to Jennifer from her tribe the Tuhoe. It is said the Patupaiarehe can still be found deep in the forests or mist covered hill tops. How exciting a new race of people I knew nothing about. I was searching for more. More about myself, more about life, and more importantly home. After all these years in Australia I still had not found home. Excitably I mapped out my trek for the central north island of New Zealand.

I boarded the plane, anticipating my wilderness adventure. On arrival a great flood of emotion poured out of me, knowing in my heart I had found home. I felt raw and open. Tears streamed down my cheeks. I felt a connection like no other. I sobbed. I was taken back at how overwhelmed I felt about this place I had scarcely seen yet. After a good night's sleep it was time to hit the road, in search of a better understanding of the area. I made my way to Tongariro National Park where the second major earth chakra lay. I trekked through bush tracks which led me to a rise. I could see shimmering water peeping through the trees. My heart opened with excitement. I had made it. I said "Hello", like I had been reacquainted with a long lost friend. The closer I got the more beautiful the view became. I was in awe at how magical this area was. A stunning mountain as its backdrop, with a shimmering green lake at its feet. It was a captivating sight. I had packed light snacks, warm gear and a poncho raincoat. I planned to spend the whole day there just absorbing my surroundings. I set up my little day camp, with a tarp on the wet sand nestled into the treeline of the shore. I had my poncho on to protect against the intermittent showers. It was eerie being so far away from civilisation. I set down my two favourite crystals. A small amethyst in front of me and a carved, amber, Kwan Yin replica behind me for protection. I decided the best way to absorb the feel of this place would be to meditate. I sat cross-legged, eyes closed, but I could relax. I tried so hard to let go, but I could felt a rush of energy coming toward me like a bull. I opened my eyes, turned around, nothing, no-one to be seen. Okay just relax I thought, shrug it off, it is just nature. I then heard a male voice chanting and with that came a vision. A brute man appeared. He had a tattooed face, with protruding eyes, peering in my direction from a short distance away in the scrub. I then saw a woman coming toward me. She had long dark straight hair bearing a tattooed chin. Both apparitions were skulking towards me like an ambush. Now I felt really uneasy. I tried to communicate with them mentally obout my peaceful intentions, to no avail. In that same moment a duck waddled up toward me from the lake shore. The duck picked up my small amethyst crystal that I had in front of me. He then waddled back down to the lake shore and dropped my crystal into the water. A sense of ease came over me. "Oh an offering", I thought, "I needed to give an offering". Once this happened and had been recognized by me, the energies of the lake subsided. My surroundings became quiet and peace fell around me. I went back to my meditation, after thanking this wise little duck, who befriended my spirit. Two rainstorms danced in front of me. Their low lying fog passed like time-lapse photography. I became more nestled into the sounds of the area. The water that lapped on the shore. The wind that tunnelled and rose through the trees like the sound of steam, as it drew closer. Bird families echoing their chorus and positions to one another. Then came the silence. Within the silence the majestic mountain felt like an anchor grounding me in contentment. I became peckish, so I pulled out my snacks of nuts, seeds, and dried fruit. To my surprise the duck returned. I was happy to have the company after many hours alone. The duck was so tame. It sat next to me and ate out of my hand. I decided to call my feathered friend Percy. It was getting late into the afternoon and the weather was becoming bleak once more. I decided to leave and give thanks to this picture perfect place, in search of civilisation once again. There was such a magnetic pull in this area. Each step back along the track felt like I was leaving wonderland. Halfway down the track a small bird was chirping urgently. I stopped to see it roost on the tree next to me, at eye level. It looked at me chirping madly. I felt honoured for such a directly intimate connection. I chirped back, as you do, then went to take a step forward. The little bird swooped down onto the ground in front of me. It looked up at me from the path still chirping importantly. Rain started to fall and at that moment I decided to stay in the little town I had passed on my way to the lake. The bird then flew away. A sense of gratitude came over me. How beautiful that moment was. Wow, I felt privileged. I made it back to the car and reminisced on my days beautiful adventure. My tummy grumbled for food. I found a low-budget room, in the little town of Turangi for the night. I asked the owner where there was a good place to eat. I was directed to the Club in town.

I was famished and ordered a serve of Bangers & Mash. I sat out the back with my journal writing about my experiences so far. A tiny Maori lady came outside and introduced herself as Auntie Val. She asked where I was from. I told her Australia. She asked "Are you on your own"? I replied "Yes". She replied "You are brave". Auntie Val asked what brought me to New Zealand. I said "The nature of this area and the children of the mist, the little people, I hope to see them as well, my Maori sis in Australia told me about them". Auntie Val giggled. She said "That is what I am, I am a child of the mist". Auntie Val asked the name my Maori sis. I told her Jennifer's surname and her face lit up. It was Auntie Val's Grandfathers surname. They were related to each other through their ancestry. Tuhoe was home to the children of the mist, where both Jennifer and Aunty Val were from. A land steeped in heritage, folklore, and mystery. It is told that some Maori were descendants of the Patupaiarehe or known as children of the mist. Legend says that the union of Patupaiarehe with mortal woman created Maori people with red hair and fair complexions. I went on to tell Auntie Val of my day. All of it. The tribal man and woman, to the duck that showed me I needed to give an offering. It was great as Auntie Val confirmed my vision and feelings of the area. The two apparitions I saw were guardians of that area. The woman, a queen of sorts and the man her guardian. Auntie Val agreed about the duck, letting me know that an offering is always needed when entering these natural places. "It doesn't need to be anything special, even a leaf or feather, it is your intention that matters", she said. It was so good to know. This was the sort of information I was after. I really wanted to know this land, its people and traditions.

Auntie Val said "My son who lives in Australia, he is working as an engineer". I replied "Where in Australia?" Auntie Val told me the name of a small country town.

I gasped for breathe. "That is where I was born", I said. o I was in shock at this coincidence. After that connection Auntie Val made me feel like family. She introduced me to all the other patrons. I felt this was a good omen and that I was meant to be here. Auntie Val introduced me to her nephew James. A man with long dark hair and unassuming in character. Auntie Val was thrilled to introduce me as a girl from Australia that was born in the town where her son worked. James and Auntie Val's son grew up together. We exchanged pleasantries and he sat down a few chairs away from me. Everyone left to go inside except the two of us. He came too sat across from me. He asked "Do you play 8 ball?" I answered "Yes, but I am not very good". Here's me thinking him and I would just have a friendly game, but no. My name goes up on the board for the 8 ball tournament that night. I lost after my third game. I rallying with the locals from young to old. It was fun and I felt comfortable. Everyone was so friendly. James fleetingly stopped to interact and exchange stories with me. I got to know he was a sailor in his younger years. He sailed the world, but missed home. I understood. "It is so beautiful here", I said. I told James my story of visiting the lake. James didn't even know where it was. He was perplexed that a tourist found a place he had not heard of, in his own town. I gave him directions and expressed how magical it was. James was lovely, humble, gentle and courteous, I felt safe. I decided to leave after such a long day. I said my goodbyes to all I had met. James asked if I was interested in attending a family dinner the following night. I looked at him puzzled, thinking I have just met you. James hurriedly explained that it was his niece's birthday on that night. He said it was a family gathering and assured me that his family was nice. I did say to him that I was keen to get to know the locals and what it was like to live here. He gave me his number and said have a think about it. James offered to walk me to my car, which I thought was very gentlemanly of him. He said "I may never see you again, can I give you a hug?" I thought a hug is tame. On arrival at my room I looked forward to resting my weary bones. I got into bed to hear the pulsating screech of a cricket. I turned on the light to hunt for it, to no avail. I thought it would be much happier outside and so would I if I could find it. I got to the stage where the moments of silence between the pulsating screeches of the cricket were my resting point. Rigid, rest, rigid, rest. It is funny when a sound is repetitive enough, you get used to it and adapt. With heavy eyes and a stimulating sound I drifted off to sleep. I am not sure how long I was asleep but I woke up saying "he is the one". A picture of James swept through my mind. What he's the one?, I questioned myself, with this peculiar feeling inside of me. I still wasn't sure. How can I ignore this feeling and what I woke up saying? I laughed out loud, then an almighty siren sounded over and over, piercing the whole town. I became frightened What did the siren mean? I was holidaying in a volcanic area, prone to eruptions. Was this one? I decided to stay in my room. Surely someone would come and get me if this was an emergency, I hoped. After the longest five minutes of my life, the siren stopped. All was quiet again, except for the noise of the cricket. What a night. I had little rest, with amazing connections and I may have found my love? How ridiculously wonderful. I fell back to sleep from exhaustion. I woke determined not to spend another night in this noisy motel. I packed up my things and made my way into town to find better accommodation. Nothing jumped out at me in my drive. There were no motels, I only saw the bakery. I decided to stop in for some breakfast. I got a pastry and sat outside to eat. A boy greeted me who was a friend of James's. I had met him the night before. His name was Henry. He sat down for a brief chat. I asked him about the siren I had heard last night. Henry said "It is was an alarm to tell the emergency services and townsfolk that there has been an accident not far from town". I said "I thought it was a volcanic eruption warning, but no one knocked on my door to evacuate me, so I figured it was ok". We laughed. After he left I thought about James and his invitation to his niece's birthday party. I was still undecided. It was a gamble. I didn't know James from a bar of soap. What if he turned out to be an axe murderer or something? I decided to visit the tourist information centre and find a more suitable, quiet room. I found a lovely place just across town. It was quiet, clean and boy was I tired! I tested the bed to find myself waking up three hours later. It was mid-afternoon. I had to make a decision about tonight. I thought what the hell, I will go. It will give me a good bearing on what makes this town tick. I rang the number, nervously. No one answered. I left a message accepting James's invitation and I let him know where I was staying. I asked if he could let me know what time and where. I had a shower and got ready. There was still no reply from him. I started second guessing the whole encounter. I decided to go to the motel restaurant to see what they had for dinner. The desk clerk said "You have a missed call from James, he asked if you can call him, and he was sorry he missed your call. My spirit lightened. I wasn't wrong in my judgement of character, he was a decent man. I walked back to my room and saw a green station wagon driving off from the grounds. That was him I thought. I rang his number again. James answered in a friendly manner. He said "I have just come from your motel". I replied "Is your car green". He said "Yes, how did you know". I said "Something inside of me said it was you, as I saw the car drive off". He asked "Do you still want to come to his niece's birthday?" I said "Yes, do you want me to drive there?" "No, I will come and pick you up it will be easier". He arrived and opened the car door for me in a chivalrous manner and we went on our way. I was a little apprehensive and felt vulnerable, I thought, oh well if worst comes to worst I can always catch a taxi back to the motel. Luckily James was a pure gentleman. His family were not unlike my own and a fun night was had by all. Everyone was so accommodating and friendly. James escorted me back to the motel when I was ready. We sat out the front of my motel unit on a clear starlit night.

We talked for hours. I was blown away at the heart felt delivery of his experiences. He told me quite personal, intimate details. Even he was shocked to be sharing the experiences with me. I felt a sense of warmth through my torso, from my belly to my chest, like nothing I had felt before. My mum used to say I would know when it is true love, I would feel it. Is this what she meant? I listened intently, captured by every word. His mouth, his eyes, and his skin, captured I was. He graciously parted and thanked me for the nice night, I agreed. I said "I would like to see you again". We made plans to go into town the next day. He was to be my tour guide for the local sights. He gave me his address. I picked him up mid-morning the next day. That day I was treated to more than just sight-seeing. James told me the history and Maori legends on how this land was made. It made each area have more depth and feeling. My interest sparkled like a child in wonder. Moments of warmth were exchanged in glimpses between us. The more I got to know James, the more my former intuition felt true. He is the one. It was too early to be sure, but boy, oh boy, it was shaping up that way. Even though we were strangers our connection was care-free, open and lovely. We only had a few days together before I travelled back to Australia. My time was so magical. I wondered whether he felt it too. We exchanged numbers and admitted how familiar we had become to each other. We were taken with each other. A bond had formed. How strong was it going to be with so many miles apart? With our goodbye regretful. I didn't want to leave him, or the mountains and the land I now felt connected to. Tears ran down my cheeks as the plane took off. Will I ever see you again? I thought. I arrived home and I was perplexed at all I had experienced in New Zealand. It was almost like a dream now. I tried to call James on the number he gave me, but alas to no avail. There was a problem with the international area code. I had almost given up when I received a call from James. I was so happy. I told him of the trouble I had contacting him. He too had the same problem. I told him how glad I was he had called. "I thought I had lost you", I said. I felt a little embarrassed with what just came out of my mouth. "Oops I hope that's not too much", I said. James went on to tell me about the feeling he has had since the day I left. He said "I really like you". Phew, I didn't make a fool of myself. I thought. I agreed in return of his feelings. I told him that I have never felt like this before. We talked regularly on the phone which strengthened our bond. It became like torture after a while. I asked

"When I am going to see you again?" James replied "What if I come for a visit, a holiday". I said "Yes please, that would be lovely". The arrangements were made, he was coming. When he arrived it was like meeting an old friend. It was so relaxed, fun and exciting. It was my turn to show him around. It was such a joyous time. Love grew between us as each day became more special. When we parted again for the second time, what had grown between us now felt so stretched. It hurt to be without each other. My independent, reliable life, now became unstable. My whole life was altered. Time passed. Our phone conversations grew deeper, stronger. The pull for us to be together outweighed our existence. I decided to leave all that was familiar to me and move to New Zealand to be with him. James came back to Australia to take me home to New Zealand. Little did I know he would ask me to marry him? I became his fiancé. James proposed to me at the beach on a warm spring day. My fears and worries about moving to a new land subsided. My home now was with James.

Chapter 16

My friend Jennifer put me onto a spiritual site from New Zealand. A site dedicated to the sharing and awakening of seer's prophets and healers of this land. Spirituality was a way of life here. I felt instant comfort, relief, and excitement of what was to come. There was an event advertised on the site for an International gathering of healers on the north island. I felt this was an omen, seeing as I had just arrived. I thought what a great way to meet like-minded people. It was hosted at a local Maori meeting house called a Marae. It came with all the trimmings of Maori tradition and culture.

James was unable to join me on this occasion due to work commitments. I was flying solo. This was fine as I felt it was something I had to do on my own. I wanted to truly understand and feel the Maori culture, without influence. It was a test, a challenge, but most of all a way to find out if I can adjust to this new life in New Zealand.

I packed myself and my dog Rusty on a five hours drive inland, to our destination. I arrived in what felt like the middle of nowhere. No shops, only a handful of houses and the Marae. I parked under a tree, next to a man sleeping on the ground. He woke with a smile. We introduced ourselves and then went on to meet others of the same ilk. I was referred to as sister on meeting them. I immediately felt a part of this gathering of strangers. I found out later through our varying talks, teachings and meetings, how alike we all were. A common thread between us. The call of Papatuanuku (mother earth) to heal ourselves, our rifts and this land. It was there I met Mathew. He became my connector to further gatherings of like-minds the Patupaiarehe or faerie people. He and I clashed energies to start with. Once we were comfortable with each other, he exchanged knowledge of some sacred sites on the north island. Mathew told me he was attending one of these sites in the coming months. He asked if I would be interested in meeting the Patupaiarehe/faerie people. I excitably said "Yes please, I have heard about them through my Maori sis Jennifer". We exchanged contact details then went on to enjoy the weekend gathering.

On the second last day it was announced that we needed to vacate the Marae into the adjacent sleeping quarters. There had been a death in the local community. A tangi (Maori funeral) was being held there for the whanau (family) the next morning. We were asked to join the local custodians of the Marae (meeting house) to welcome the grieving whanau (family). I was apprehensive, but happy to help the hosts of the local Marae (meeting house) in return for their hospitality.

The next morning I was unsure of the protocol needed. We were talked through what was expected of us. It was more or less a silent vigil to represent the Marae (local custodians of the meeting house) in welcoming on the whanau (family). Once the grieving whanau (family) had been sung onto the Marae (meeting house), we each took a turn individually greeting each person. This was done in a line one after the other. You either gave a kiss on the cheek or a hongi. (Maori greeting done by pressing noses and foreheads together to exchange the breath of life). It was after this that the energy changed from light, happy, and inquisitive, to sombre, dark, and at times frightening. We all left the whanau (family) to grieve. We set about our day's teachings and connections. We all sat on a large open grassed area behind the buildings to commence our earth ceremony. Individual blessings were given to each and every one of us. An appointed woman used a mixture of dirt and water, from the nearby stream to anoint our third eye. This was done to connect us all to Papatuanuku (mother earth). A world prayer was then sent out in unity from us, to the earth and all its inhabitants. Scattered through us were some of the grieving whanau (family). Their energy angry and stoic. I felt the energy and justified it by the fact they had just lost a loved one. They had no idea why we were all gathered there, or what we were doing. The ceremony finished. I got up to move because the energy was making me feel uncomfortable. I looked for some of the new friends I had met, but to no avail. I walked and was followed by two girls. Everywhere I walked they were giving me evil stares from a distance. I did not feel safe. The only faces I saw were ones I did not know. Their wrath toward me was *so strong that I felt compelled to leave. I thanked the organizers briefly and then ran into Mathew. I asked him to pass on my apologies to the others that I had met. I explained to him that I had to go. He asked "Are you alright?" "Not really", I answered. I explained to Mathew that since the Tangi (Maori funeral) the energy had changed. It was not very nice anymore, and that I didn't feel safe. Mathew explained that there were some people throwing knives at other people's backs. I said that is exactly what it feels like. I said "Especially two girls in particular". I said "Everywhere I go they are there watching me, staring". He said "Why do you think I stick so close to the Kaumatua's (Maori elders) no one throws knives at them". The elders held great mana equalling supernatural force and were of high authority within the Maori community. He said "It is ok, you leave if you feel you need to, I will tell the others goodbye for you". I thanked him. Mathew said "Just quickly before you go, I must tell you this". "When you get home, lie on the ground outside and scan your body for daggers". "If you find any, don't just pull them out". "You will have to turn them anti-clockwise, then pull them out, otherwise you will tear holes in your auric field". "When you have pulled the first one out there will be a hole". "You will need to fill it up again with light energy". He went on to say "Don't be surprised if you find more than one dagger, as there is usually a few of them". He said "Once you have done this, and you think you have removed them all, scan again, the same way, the next morning, just to be sure you haven't missed any". I thanked him with my trusting heart. Mathew really understood what had happened to me. I was uplifted and relieved to finally make it home with my trusty dog Rusty.*

I laid outside on the back lawn and scanned my body. One, two, three, four, five, six, knives I pulled out of my auric field. I was amazed. I understood fully why I was feeling so uncomfortable. I rested that night like one thousand sleeps in one. I woke and went outside to scan my auric field again. I found another five daggers to remove. It was as if they were layered into my energy field. I wondered how I could bring up so much resentment in another. I did not know. I took my dog and myself to the river for a walk. We cleansed ourselves with the water. I felt grounded, clear, and at peace once again.

The next morning my higher self said "We are going to a special place today". I wondered how I would know where to go. I was told to drive

15 kilometres out of town. I kept watch on the odometer reading. I felt inspired to stop after 10 kilometres. I drove down to a marina. This is not 15 kilometres. I heard in my mind. Ok keep driving. I wondered where the heck I was going. "Trust", I said. It was nearing 15 kilometres on the odometer when I was told turn. I turned into the street as I was cornering the bend. I parked the car, as close as I could get to the lake. I had to walk through the yard of a holiday home to gain access. I went to walk left and was told no the other way. I was all excited, wondering what adventure awaited me. In front of me was a rocky point that looked out to the burial island of Motutaiko. This island had been like a magnet since my first visit in 2011. Drawing in my gaze from any point of view it could conduct. I sensed its majestic presence, even before I was told of its significance. I stood at the point and breathed in the view. I looked down into the water from the edge of my rock platform and followed it with my eyes. I saw what looked like pieces of iridescent, white chalky bones, trailing to the island. I felt like singing a tune and before I knew it I was relaying to the island my hearts sway in sound. This lasted about ten minutes. I was captivated with the islands presence and what it stirred within me. I stopped singing and started to walk back along the shore. I heard a man's voice speak. It was coming from the island. He thanked me for singing to them all. He said "No-one has sung to us for a very long time". I was honoured by his thankfulness. He asked me to come back and sing for them soon. I replied "I will". I walked away with a lightened spirit, full of wonder and awe at what I had experienced. This certainly was a special place. A couple of weeks passed before I was called back. I walked the lake shore toward the point and heard the same man say "There is something I want to show you". The lake was calm as I connected to the point and the area around me. I was told to lay down. There were large flat rock shelves covering the point. I laid down on one of them to then tune in as best I could. My eyes were closed, but I could hear nothing. I started to feel uneasy, like something wasn't right. I looked past the Island to the ever rising lake horizon. Out the back it was becoming rough, while around me the lake was calm. Before I knew it the lake chopped up and the wind began to swirl. I looked down at the rock shelf I was lying on and saw blood. This spooked me, so I left. As I walked up the shore with the ever increasing turbulent waves, wind and bad weather. I wondered if I had done something wrong. I was not sure if I had offended

the ancestors. I asked if I had done anything wrong. I looked down and saw a green marbled rock in the shape of a heart. Then I heard the male voice say "This is for you". I replied "Thank you", with an eased heart. That was enough to confirm that everything was ok. Sometime after, I spoke with a Maori woman from the local area. She alerted me to the fact, that where I stood on the rock shelf, was where they used to prepare the dead for burial on the island. It all made sense now.

James returned home the next day after working a month at sea. I was so happy to have him home and to share my experiences. James was hurt for me, after hearing about daggers being thrown at me from the spiritual gathering. He wanted to cheer me up. James asked if he could take me to his tribal homeland of Tuhoe, which is nestled in the Urewera ranges. I agreed. James wanted to visit his sister and her family who live in the area. We decided we would stay with her and then go camping. I was excited to meet James's sister and explore the area of the children in the mist. A week before Christmas we packed the car and our trusty dog Rusty for this magical adventure. It was a long five hour drive, so we took our time. I started coming down with cold like symptoms the first couple of hours into the drive. I brushed it off. A runny nose and sneezing wouldn't hamper the trip. We decided to stop and sleep the night half way to the Urewera. During the night, my so called cold, turned into a flu. I woke that morning with a horrendously sore head. I was all blocked up, and had aches all through my body. James was so determined to keep going that he disregarded my worsening symptoms. The more we drove, the more sick I became. All I wanted to do was rest in bed. I had to tell James that I couldn't go. I was not well enough. Begrudgingly James rang his sister to tell her we would not be coming. I went to bed as soon as we arrived home. I dreamt that night of a group of Maori people. They were simply dressed, and some wearing traditional flax attire. They were all vying to see me and said "We don't know who you are". I woke that morning and told James about my dream. He said "Oh no". I asked "What does it mean". He said "You need to be blessed into the family, I need to tell them you are going to be my wife". It was the ancestors of his whanau (family). James said "That is why you got sick". I didn't understand. "Why" I asked. "Because you are not from my land and had not been given permission", he replied. James said "I know what to do". He asked me to go to the river and get some water to do a blessing with. While I was gone James got out the whanau's whakapapa (list of family ancestral lineage). He also got a green stone, sacred to New Zealand in the form of a pendant necklace. It was given to him by the sister we were going to visit for Christmas. He first lay the full table length whakapapa out. I sat on one side of the paper and James on the other side. He held my hands over the top of the pages and we motioned across the length of the ancestral list. He evoked the ancestors, then proceeded to tell them that I was going to be his wife. He asked them to accept me into the family and to bless our union. Tears welled in my eyes. James then asked me to come outside. I was to hold our engagement rings and the taonga (Maori gift) which was the green stone pendant necklace in my outstretched hand. James then used the water from the river to bless them and me as one of the whanau (family). Tears ran down my cheeks. I told James that I could feel the difference now. I started to feel better. I made a joke saying "There is always next year". We smiled at each other.

Chapter 17

I received a txt from Mathew, whom I met months earlier at my first spiritual gathering in Aotearoa, New Zealand. He invited me to a gathering at Pureora Forest to see real life faeries, the Patupaiarehe or also known as little people. I was ecstatic at the invitation. I asked what to bring. All I needed to bring was warm clothes, bedding and food to share. Done.

I dreamt that night of two little people. A male and a female with sandy blonde hair and pale skin. They were small in stature, no more than 60 centimetres high, with a wiry build. Their clothing was made of plant fibre, which was fashioned into a skirt kilt for the male, and a dress for the female. The male was holding a tall stick and talking. He was not talking with his mouth but with his eyes and mind, which relayed to my mind. A lot was being said by him, and seemed jumbled to my ears from the hurried speech. My attention travelled behind him to the female. She was cupping her face, with her back turned to me. I felt she was coy, shy, and confronted by this meeting. I woke in the morning remembering what I had experienced in my dream. They were trying to tell me something, but I couldn't work out what. I was excited to know what they looked like, and even more excited for the upcoming trip to Pureora forest.

Mathew was kind enough to meet me at home and escort me to Pureora. It was a two and a half hour drive there. It was tricky to find if you had not been there before. We got closer to the forest turn off when it started to drizzle. The scenery had changed from flat farmlands to rocky hills and valleys that were covered in native bush. We turned down a dirt road that rose and winded around for about five kilometres. I saw in my mind's eye a group of little people. One in particular a male, running at speed in the bush alongside the car. He was telepathically saying to the others, "They're here, they're here", excitedly. It was the same little man I saw in my dream the night before. I was excited but also a little apprehensive, as I was coming onto their turf now. I did not know what was to come.

A quaint weatherboard lodge appeared over the rise, nestled amongst a small clearing surrounded by native forest. There was a rough brick barbeque fire, next to a round concrete table with matching concrete pillar stools. Two men of Maori decent were already there. They were in their late 50's. I was introduced first to Will. A gentle man with charisma, who made you feel up beat in his presence. He was holding a stick intricately carved with pictures that had a magnificent quartz crystal on top. I was intrigued by it and asked him who had made his stick. A close relation of Will's had carved it for him. It was the story of creation from the base, to the top of the stick. Will said "This sort of decorative stick is called a rakau or talking stick. Will made a joke by saying "I use it mainly to hold myself up these days, because of my bad legs", he laughed. Will was so humble and approachable.

The other man was Will's good friend Reginald. A very unassuming person, almost reserved, upon my first impression. I came to realise that Reginald did not speak unless he had something profound to share.

Mathew enlightened me that Will was the Kaumatua (respected elder) that helped put this gathering together. Will had been coming to Pureora for years to regularly connect back to the spirit of the surrounding lands and the Patupaiarehe, known as faerie folk or little people.

The lodge had four dorms, laden with bunk beds. They slept up to twenty-five people. There was a big, fully equipped kitchen and dining room. There was a separate ablution blocks for men and women. Tents could also be erected on the grassy area outside surrounding the lodge if preferred. It was so nice to be away from civilization, and in such a tranquil setting.

Mathew asked if I would like to share one of the dorms with him and his friend Tonya. I agreed. We then went about setting up our bedding in the sleeping area. Mathew said "I will bless the room by sprinkling water around the outside". "The room that we are in usually gets a lot of activity at night", Mathew said. I inquisitively asked "What sort of activity?" he replied "Knocking on the windows, footsteps, sticks banging together, singing". This excited and un-nerved me at the same time. I was oh so thankful that I was not in there alone.

Another good friend of Will's arrived named Gareth. On first glance Gareth's features reminded me of a garden gnome. He was short in stature with a stocky build. He had shoulder length white hair and a long white beard. He had a cheerful appearance that surrounded friendly eyes. Unbeknownst to me he was there to shoot a documentary film about the little people of the forest, the Patupaiarehe. There was a film crew coming up from Auckland that day. Gareth has been coming to Pureora for years and spoke of different memorable encounters with the little people. He had heard the sound of sticks clanging together in the surrounding forest at night, also flutes playing, giggling, laughing, and the singing, like that of small children. Gareth's interest stemmed from his many years of research into the sacred sites and ancient mysteries of Aotearoa, New Zealand. It was all so wildly exciting. I felt like a child again anticipating the unexpected adventure that awaited us. Gareth and Will, both painted us a vivid picture of what to expect that night.

Will announced that before anyone ventured into the forest a Karakia (prayer) needed to be done. This was done to pay homage to the forest elementals and also the ancestors of the area. Will explained that it prepares and announces to the spirits of the land our intention and presence. This in turn will keep us all safe, especially when walking through the forest. We had to wait for the others to arrive from Auckland. I was content to have that little bit of extra time to get used to my surroundings. After a short while the film crew arrived from Auckland. We introduced ourselves to one another in welcoming each person one by one. They were a young group in their twenties and thirties. Moments after their arrival another couple turned up. They were in their 40's. They were gypsy-like. They both travelled all over New Zealand to attend spiritual events and places of interest. We all started chatting and getting to know each other. The film crew asked us to re-enact our initial welcome introductions for the film. We all agreed. I felt the challenge of making it look natural for the second time round.

Once the newcomers were settled in, Will rallied us all up for a walk into the forest. Will explained to the newcomers that he would be doing a Karakia (prayer) before entering the forest and the reasons behind it.

Will told us that doing a karakia (prayer) before entering any natural area was a tradition from the past. He went on to say that is rarely practised today and so because of this, it is being forgotten. This knowledge is not being passed down to our mokopuna (children) and it is in real danger of being lost forever.

Will went on to tell us that he was singled out from his many siblings, to be taught the traditional old ways. He did not understand why he had to sit and listen to the old people, while his brothers and sisters were free to play. Not until he was older and could understand what was taught, did he realize he was not punished, but privileged to be chosen. After this short and meaningful korero (talk) we exited the lodge to start on our trail.

My head tingled like a pin cushion with hundreds of tiny pulsing holes. My body felt light and floating. I mentioned this state out aloud to Gareth. He smirked and said "Are you sensitive?" I replied "Very". Gareth said "There is a lot of different energies out here". My head throbbed and pulsed as we stopped to hear Will's karakia (prayer). Will's breathe echoed through every crevice and nook in the forest. A strong, loud, honourable presence, that made you feel safe to be with him. A mirage of elders appeared to his left, guardians cloaked as one energy, holding the integrity of this place. Will's words folded back into the surrounding scenery. Now appeased with the karakia (prayer) we walked slowly through the forest. Will pointed out different plants with their medicinal, healing and nourishment qualities along the way. There was so much to take in. Every cell of my body felt like open funnels, like that of natural honeycomb. Everything around me had a presence. The ground, the sky, the trees, plants, insects, and birds, pulsing with substance. This in turn made me feel a part of everything.

Will led us half the way until we reached a giant Matai tree. This tree is said to be the keeper of knowledge from that area. The original keeper of knowledge was a grandmother tree that perished in a fire about a decade earlier. She passed her knowledge onto this giant Matai brother for safe keeping. Will spoke of the grandmother tree as an old friend, sadly missed but never forgotten. I pondered on the changes the ole girl would have witnessed in her time. I wondered how long she and the present knowledge keeper had been standing. I looked in awe at the strength, size, and grandeur of the tree's surrounding us. Will returned to the lodge to rest his legs, while the rest of us carried along the forty minute circle path back to the lodge. The film crew lingered at the site next to the tree of knowledge, to gage their set up for that nights filming. Their hope was to catch supernatural phenomena or little people on camera, for their movie.

It was decided over dinner that evening to venture back to the forest around 3am. Will said "It is the best and most likely time to witness unusual occurrences in the area from the Patupaiarehe". (Faerie folk, little people) It is believed that this is when they are most active, due to the veil of night, and also in dense fog to hide from view.

We all shared our tales and expectations, along with knowledge on the history and behaviours of the Patupaiarehe. (Faerie folk, little people)

I heard that they don't like cooked food, preferring to eat raw food. It was also said that they are afraid of bright light.

Will shared stories that evening from his childhood, about playing with the Patupaiarehe. (Faerie folk, little people) The story was recurrent each nightfall until his adolescence. He would be woken by the Patupaiarehe (Faerie folk, little people) calling his name and knocking on the window of his room. He was not frightened as they were his playmates. Will would spend all night with them playing stick games, singing, dancing, jumping, and spinning, like acrobats. He knew all the Patupaiarehe (Faerie folk, little people) clan from old to young, just like his own family. Will said that in his day they did not wear pyjamas to bed. Most of the Patupaiarehe (Faerie folk, little people) were also naked, apart from natural fibres worn more as adornments than clothing. When daylight beckoned, his playmates the Patupaiarehe (Faerie folk, little people) would try to encourage Will to come home with them. Their home was behind a waterfall, not far from where they all played together. Will sensed that if he went with them, past the waterfall that he would not be able to come back. Will would always decline their invitation. His excuse to them was that he had to go back to his own family. This story intrigued me. Here was a man almost sixty years old who candidly shared what most people would think was impossible. A time in his life that still made his eyes sparkle in its telling. The joy and delight shared by Will of this time, raised the vibration of all those listening. The wonder, and the imagination. All was set free once again. This helped us to rekindle our childlike eyes.

I decided to have a smoke before retiring to bed for our early 3am wake up call. I walked out to the carport to find Mathew and Reginald had the same idea. I remembered I had left my smokes and lighter on the bench seat just around the corner between two cars. The area was shrouded in darkness. Without a thought I made my way over to retrieve them. I reached for my smokes and lighter. With my very next step I trod on the most peculiar thing. The sensation it gave me I will never forget. Automatically I apologized and flicked my lighter on. There was nothing to be seen. My mind and senses raced to compute what had just happened. It was then I knew it was one of them, the Patupaiarehe. (Faerie folk, little people) I had trodden on its foot. Excitably I rushed back to tell Mathew and Reginald what had happened. I realized from the sensation through my foot, that their skin is spongey, almost rubbery, but elastic. This would explain their ability to jump, spring and tumble as Will had told us in his stories. My first encounter with the Patupaiarehe (Faerie folk, little people) relayed so much information about them. Within that moment I also noted that they are not warm blooded. This would be another reason why were able to dress minimally all year round as Will had described. Their atomic energy fires. It is construed differently to our cells. It is like sparking fragments that join together to produce solid form, which bounce within themselves. The sparking fragments can then also bounce out of their solid, form when they want to emanate and fall back into their natural surroundings. I went to bed that night with one eye and one ear open. Thankfully I was sharing a room with Mathew, otherwise I don't think I would have got any rest. Through the night I heard sticks clanging together outside our room at irregular intervals. There was also beautiful angelic singing way off in the distance. I was almost asleep when I heard a loud bang. The dorms main door abruptly opened. Little footsteps could be heard running down the corridor. I was startled. I wondered whether anyone else had heard the noise. This seemed like my last thought when suddenly it was 3am. Everyone started getting up and readying themselves for the forest adventure.

I overheard the others talking outside, about the door opening in the night. I went outside and asked if they heard the footsteps running through the corridor. They did. Ah confirmed, I thought. Some of the girls also heard a flute playing in the night. Gareth told us that this is one of the ways the Patupaiarehe (Faerie folk, little people) lure people outside. He said "You may hear beautiful singing, flutes, and sticks clanging together or even whistling to lure you outside to investigate". I was in wonderment. How awesomely cool with a twist of uh-oh. I was tingling and ecstatic with anticipation. The group gathered outside. Will and Reginald stayed asleep in bed. The rest of us rallied together for debriefing. Two woman out of the film *crew were staying behind for a different angle on the movie. I felt I did not need to go into the forest for contact, due to the commotion we had already experienced around the lodge. A Maori lady also decided to stay and do her own connecting. We were both heckled for not wanting to go into the forest at night. All the stories we had heard of the Patupaiarehe (Faerie folk, little people) were now playing through our minds. Daunting, exciting, scary and downright bravery pulsed with every beat of our hearts. The forest troop did a head count before setting off. They checked that their long distance radios were working before setting off. "Check one, check two", they said. Within moments they trekked off into the darkness. I and the other Maori lady were drawn to opposite sides of the lodge. Both areas backed onto bush land. Darkness was ahead of me, to the left of me, and to the right of me. There was a dim light emanating from the lodge hall behind me as my backdrop. I sat there quietly in four layers of clothing for warmth. It was nearing the end of winter, but it was still thickly cold. I tuned all my senses into my surroundings. A Kaka bird called in the distance. I then heard a whistle sounding like a woo woo. Sticks then clanged twice before the sound of many footsteps ran in my direction. I realized that the Patupaiarehe (faerie folk, little people) were signalling to each other. A surge of energy came towards me from the adjacent hill. As it got closer I envisioned many forms. I noted two giants as the guardian's. They were at the front and back of the tribe of Patupaiarehe. (Faerie folk, little people) The giants alerted the others to any energy spikes deducing from our human presence. The tribe ranged from beings 15-20cm high, while others were the size as a 3-7 year old child. This image reminded me of the frightening movie "children of the corn". I quickly changed my thoughts. Fear was not a feeling I wanted to have inside of me, or to project to them. I then saw the other two woman from the film crew come and sit outside at the concrete table with the pillar stools. I could just hear them from where I was sitting. It was about 150 metres away, shrouded in darkness. I noticed them start filming and talking. This distraction was nice for me. It made me feel comfortable enough to tune into the Patupaiarehe (Faerie folk, little people) again. The energy was tense. I waited, and watched for a trigger. I took a sip of water out of my silver flask. I felt their concern about this large metal object. I said with my mind's eye, through my heart, "It is not a weapon". The energy from them turned down a couple of notches. I fed back to them telepathically that I had picked their vibration up through my head and heart. An energetic correspondence through feeling. I thanked them for coming and for not being afraid to come near me. I gave them compliments of how magical they were. I could see them scarcely dressed or wearing natural fibre sashes covering various body parts. I exclaimed to them "You must not feel the cold". I could feel how loving they were. "You pretend to be scary, so that we humans won't get close to you and hurt you, I wouldn't hurt you", I told them. "I love you, you are nice" they said. "I love you too", I replied. They asked me to come and play. The pull was magnetic. The joy and excitement inside of me was like a little ball in my chest waiting to turn. "I can't", my rational mind decreed. I had no idea what I would be in for if I accepted the invite. The little ones sulked a bit, like a sad child not getting their way. "I still want to be your friend", I said. "Maybe next time I will come and play", I said. The energy lightened as the giant guardians addressed the tribe's restlessness. A Kaka bird signalled the call as the lead on. The rest of the tribe followed with coded whistles, winding up through the valley embankment. You could hear how vast the size of the group was with the responding calls to each other. Their energy swarmed through the forest toward the other group filming deep in the forest. Now they are going to share some fun with them I thought. The rush was gone. The energy quietened, except for their racket in the far off distance. Twenty minutes or so passed. There had been no more activity. I approached the two woman filming. I asked if they had seen or heard the Patupaiarehe. (Faerie folk, little people) They replied "Yes there was a big group of them, but they all left in a hurry". One of the woman said "They are probably going to share some fun with the others now". I reiterated, "I heard them too and that is exactly what I thought". "I am a bit worried though as I haven't heard anything since, from or our group in the forest". We tried to contact the forest group with the long distance radios. There was nothing and no response for the next ten minutes. Butterflies started forming in my belly. I wondered if they were ok. We heard voices faintly coming closer from the forest. We then saw a light, it was them. Relief, safe and sound. We asked if they saw or heard anything while in the forest. Gareth said "Only the sound of clanging sticks, at different times, of which we recorded". The two woman and I all agreed that it was busy at the lodge. We told them how there was a whole group of them here. Will and Reginald woke up soon after the forest troop returned. Will told us that he heard the Patupaiarehe (Faerie folk, little people) calling his name and knocking on the window to come play. Will told them that he is an old man now, with bad legs that don't work properly anymore. Will said that they petitioned his reply by saying, "We have old men here too and they can still jump and spin". Will insisted to them that he cannot come out and play anymore. Reginald slept through the whole thing. Will said he was trying to wake his sleeping friend to hear the Patupaiarehe (Faerie folk, little people) but he wouldn't wake up.*

The next day we visited the Temple of The Four Winds. It was a short drive from the lodge. The Temple of The Four Winds is a sacred site, holding the ruins of an ancient teaching school. Will had an affinity with the area. It was a part of him. Through Will's status/spiritual force and ancestral connections we were given permission to enter this sacred place of learning. We were welcomed with song by the local tribe onto their ancestral lands. Will taught us a song to sing back to the local tribe out of respect for hosting us that day. We were all greeted individually in a procession line by the local tribe. One after another we were kissed on the cheek or given a hongi (Maori greeting where nose and forehead are pressed together to exchange the breathe of life.). As I waited to be greeted by them, I felt overwhelmed with emotion. I saw a fog of people behind the local tribe. I thought to myself it must be their ancestors. By the time I greeted the first man, I felt choked up. I was holding back tears. The woman next to him gave me a hongi. I burst into tears. I couldn't stop. The next woman said "Welcome home". With those words I felt like dropping to the ground. I really did feel like I had come back home. Once I got to the end of the welcome party, a girl from the Pureora group was standing next to me. She had been to the Temple of The Four Winds once before. She expressed to me the intense emotion that this place brought up within her the second time around. She had a pale bodied, cloth doll with her that she took everywhere. It was about 50cm tall, with the most beautifully painted eyes and face. It wore a patchwork cloth dress. Varying coloured strands of long, thin cut material were used for hair. It had a symbol painted on its third eye. She asked if I wanted a cuddle with the doll. I was feeling all emotional and nostalgic, so I accepted. I brought the doll up to my chest and gave it a cuddle. I looked back at the girl. My eyes were wide open in shock. I said "She has a heartbeat". "I know", replied the girl. I realized why the doll had gone everywhere with her and why it had pride of place to see the goings on around it. It was alive. I said this to the girl and then queried as to where she got it from. She said "An elderly woman at one of the city markets makes them, with her granddaughter". "She delegates which dolls can be sold to whom because of suitable character". I was intrigued and also asked about the symbol on the dolls forehead. The girl said "It is a channelled symbol from the star people". The grandmother who made the doll explained to the girl that the symbol gives the doll its life force. She is told what symbol to draw for each doll. The girl then went on to tell me that The Temple of The Four Winds was where the first star people landed on earth. It was then I understood why this place had such an effect on me. It was a cellular memory from another time. There were two sets of pews for seating on the open paddock. One seated the local tribe and the other was for us visitors. We sat and listened to the local tribe speak their history and heart knowing's. Will than shared our intentions of the day, with love, peace, humour, and an open heart. We were then allowed to have time to ourselves and get acquainted with the area. I was drawn to one end of the stone cross which rested on the ground amidst the paddock. It was all that could now be seen physically of the old teaching school. I laid down and meditated. Within minutes I noted there were caves underneath the cross. They tunnelled along in different directions. I proceeded down one of them and ran into a peculiar looking being. A cross between an elf, an animal, and an old coal miner. He was short in stature, but strong in psychic and physical strength. He was a guardian of the tunnels. Depending on your own innate energy, this determined which tunnel, or tunnels you could have access to. I spoke to him for a while. I asked him about the place and asked what he does. He was like a funny librarian from another world. I unburdened myself to him by sharing my hearts woes. He was very matter of fact and humorous in his delivery of outcomes. It was like the different tunnels. He showed me the future path of each choice, as if I was to make that decision. It all depended on me and which road I chose. Little did I know then, that the path I chose was only my personal outlook on life? It was not necessarily my true outcome. This was because another person's energy was also involved? If they are not headed in the same direction it can redirect outcomes. This creates a new set of circumstances and choices to make. We headed back to Pureora after this magnificent heart opening experience. Mathew and his friend Tonya had *to leave Pureora due to a prior engagement. I was a little perturbed, not by his leaving but the thought of having to stay in the room that night by myself. We all shared our experiences of the day, around the table that evening. I felt overwhelmed by the day, so I kept my story short and sweet. I gave no real outlay of what had happened. I was asked by Will if I was ok? I replied "Most of the time". We laughed. I did not stay up very late that night because of tiredness. I retired early. I fell straight to sleep. I woke in the night to the feeling of something the size of a possum, running from my shoulder, across my torso then to my legs and onto the floor. It was alarming. What was that, I thought? The door to my room was only letting in the tiniest bit of light from underneath it. I then had a small face appear in front of mine. It was all screwed up, with teeth showing, and its mouth open. It was one of them, the Patupaiarehe. (Faerie folk, little people) I was excited, with a hint of apprehension and fright. I knew that the little fellow was trying to scare me. I said with my mind to him "You are not scary, you're beautiful". He showed himself again, close to my face with a smile. "See, you look more beautiful when you smile", I said. Once he knew that I wasn't scared, the fun was over for him and he left. On waking in the morning I felt it was time to leave. I packed up my things and went out to my car to put them in. One of the car doors was ajar. I was sure that I had locked it, and it was alarmed so no-one could break in unannounced. This struck me as odd. There was nothing missing from the car and all seemed well. I said goodbye to everyone, and thanked Will for a magical time. I told him about my car door being open. He said "You might have some company coming home with you". I looked at him puzzled. Will told me of two European girls who could see the Patupaiarehe. (Faerie folk, little people) He said "They they took one back home with them, on the plane". "They popped the Patupaiarehe (Faerie folk, little people) in a box". "It jumped out accordingly when put through the airport scanner, then hopped back in the box for the plane trip". Will was happy for the European girls to take the one they did, as he was the most mischievous. Will said "I have many Patupaiarehe (Faerie folk, little people) living at my place". Will said "They do travel and there are different types all over the world". My inner child loved this thought, and with that story I set off home. Sure enough I felt two Patupaiarehe (Faerie folk, little people) in the back of the car. I forgot about them until the next winter. I was asleep with my husband next to the fire. My husband said "I was woken in the early hours of the morning by a poke in the head". "I thought it was you, but you were sound asleep". He said "When I closed my eyes I envisioned a man of very short build like a little person". Summer came round and we had another visit from them, well my husband did. It was a hot night, so my husband had thrown off the bed clothes. He had his bottom resting out the side of the bed. He was woken with a slap on the bum. His abrupt wake up also woke me. He told me he was slapped on the bottom. I laughed and said "Well they don't bother me". The Patupaiarehe (Faerie folk, little people) had a fun old time heckling him.*

I attended another gathering at Pureora the following year. This time I slept in a tent on the lawns outside. There was myself and another girl who also camped out. She was about 25 metres away from my camp. I brought two solar lights with me to put outside the tent. This would make it easier to see my camp at night. That night in my tent when the solar lights were losing charge, and dimming as much as lighting, it began. First I heard little footsteps running behind the tent. There seemed to be a good dozen or so Patupaiarehe (Faerie folk, little people) by the sound of it. I noted their presence with my thoughts. I tried to sleep. Just as I was nearly asleep the tent started shaking. They were pulling at the tie down ropes. When the solar lights came back on the movement would stop. This was unnerving. I was concerned about their intentions. It had been a year since being accustomed to this energy. I couldn't help but feel frightened. This is what delighted them and made the game fun. I would cancel the thought of them, and nearly fall back to sleep, when they would shake the tent again. They would then run off before the solar lights came back on. I got to the stage, after a few hours, where I was so exhausted, that I just wanted them to stop. My nerves were shot from almost falling asleep, then being rattled by them shaking the tent. I became disgruntled and said out aloud "Right that is enough, it is not funny anymore, I am going to sleep, go away". Once my fear became anger they left. It was no fun for them anymore. The next morning I asked the woman just up from me if she heard anything. She also heard the footsteps in the night, but they didn't rattle her tent. The next day two new girls arrived. They also set up a tent to sleep in that night. I said nothing of what had happened to me the night before. Sure enough the next morning I asked how the new girls slept. They too had the same occurrence of the Patupaiarehe (Faerie folk, little people) shaking the tent.

One of the girls said that she heard them whispering over and over "Come out and play, come out and play". She told them that she was too tired to play, and they left.

After breakfast a few of us sat outside. We got chatting about underground world news and events. That is where I first heard of N.E.S.A.R.A. (National Economic Security and Recovery Act). A movement in reformation of the current banking system which allows equality, fairness and monetary gain for all. I then overheard Reginald talking to another lady about the two red suns I went over and interrupted. I said "Two red suns, do you know about them". Reginald looked at me for more information. I told him and the lady to whom he was talking, about my first vision when I was 19, of two red suns. I said "I wasn't sure how this could happen". I mentioned that I saw the whole atmosphere in an ember like colour. I wasn't sure if it was going to happen from fires or a severe dust storm. That was all I could put it down to. I asked Reginald "So what is it"? I smiled in amazement that my vision had reality. Reginald said "The star Betelgeuse is going to supernova at any time". "It is far enough away from the earth not to harm our planet, yet close enough to have an effect on our skies". "The exploded Betelgeuse and our own sun will give the appearance of two red suns in the sky". "This in turn will make our skies so bright that night will not be seen for a couple of weeks". "This natural phenomena has been predicted to occur anytime from now and the next million years", he said. "I can vouch it will be in my lifetime, why else would I have seen it in a vision", I said. Wow how exciting, I thought. I love spending time with those of open minds and hearts, you exchange so much, and it's exhilarating for the spirit. Yet another magical time was had, sharing our knowing, spirit and gifts with one another. There was always a real collective of differing nationalities, characters, minds and hearts. That was what I loved about my trips to Pureora, the unity and diversity we shared. Will accepted each and every one of us on a heart level. He was not interested in the differences between us, just our spirit and hearts intention to share our souls. Will was like the winder on a jewellery box. He would turn and turn until you opened up to sing your tune. There was no competitiveness or personal goals, it was all about sharing and caring for each other's uniqueness. He could spark even the dimmest light with his presence. I adored him like a grandfather.

It was about 6 months after this that I was contacted in relation to Will's health decline. I rang Will on the phone to see if he was ok. He was talking about attending a Hui (gathering) in Australia. The way he was talking and his plans for the future, threw me off his imminent death.

We were all called to attend Will's tangi (funeral). There was a spectacularly large crowd in attendance that day. Many stories were exchanged of this humble yet larger than life character we all grew to love and respect. A sacred ceremonial cloak made of black feathers was draped across his coffin. We were all lead up the hill to the place of his burial. When Will was lowered, so was my heart with him. He made me feel like I belong in Aotearoa, New Zealand. He welcomed me into his family with an open heart and arms. He gifted me truth and belief of my path. He saw my future and the choices that I had to make. He remained neutral, understanding and without judgement. His soul was my feathery pillow to rest on. He too can now rest his weary legs. I silently cried for his loss, with my right hand over my heart in honour of the spirit he shared with us. Next thing I notice the mountain across the road in the not too far off distance. I see Wills spirit, he was naked running up the hill, full speed, yelling "I can do anything now". I heard these words echo with so much joy and mischief, just like a Patupaiarehe. (Faerie folk, little people) This vision lifted my spirits into the sky and the infinite world, he was now a part of. There has been further gatherings at Pureora since Will's passing. It was good to try and rekindle, with memory, what was started there. Except that I feel the heart is now gone. The transmission of Will's original frequency is now out of tune. We are finding it hard to gain the same wavelength that danced through each of our souls with connective acceptance.